PRACTICAL WRITING TECHNIQUES

Fifth Edition

Zan Dale Robinson, Ph.D.

SIMON & SCHUSTER
CUSTOM PUBLISHING

Printed in the United States of America

This publication has been printed using selections as
they appeared in their original format. Layout and
appearance will vary accordingly.

10 9 8 7 6 5 4 3 2 1

ISBN 0–536–58887–2
BA 6967

SIMON & SCHUSTER CUSTOM PUBLISHING
160 Gould Street/Needham Heights, MA 02194
Simon & Schuster Education Group

COPYRIGHT ACKNOWLEDGMENTS

ACKNOWLEDGMENTS

I wish to thank Donald C. Kilburn, President, Kathy Kourian, Senior Editor, Jon Miller, Associate Editor, Jeanne Rodrigues, Officer Manager and Julianna Crosier, Production Editor, all of Simon & Schuster Custom Publishing, for their advice, expertise, and unselfish assistance during the preparation of this book. Much appreciation goes to JChris Senden of Buffalo State College for his suggestions regarding student interests and reactions. I want to give special thanks to my wife, friend, and colleague, Patricia, who carefully edited and made minor revisions to the manuscript wherever necessary. It was her help and support that made it possible for me to write this book, which I dedicate to her, our children, and our grandchildren.

Because of the design of this book, which is to introduce practical writing techniques as simply as possible, I found it more pragmatic to use the male pronoun "he" rather than "he or she" whenever referring to the writer. I have done this to facilitate the idea of simplicity. I am aware of the role that gender plays in language, and I acknowledge the importance of the he/she pronoun reference. Some readers may misconstrue this design. However, my intention is solely to promote simplicity of style for the benefit of the practical writer.

CONTENTS

FOREWORD

The topic of writing has been the focus of numerous authors who over the years have produced a profusion of textbooks on how to confront this most difficult subject area. Dr. Zan Dale Robinson has written a truly simplified and useful book. He has taken a responsible and pragmatic approach to the subject of writing, and his book, *Practical Writing Techniques,* is based on his many years of firsthand teaching experience in the college classroom. Robinson's book is easy to read and understand, and includes excellent examples of the writing process along with a section about modern technical writing. It is positively the very best book that I have read in all my years of teaching regarding the subject of writing methods and techniques. I highly recommend this work for both the novice and professional writer. It is loaded with practical tips about how to write effectively.

Patricia M. McNaney
Department of English
State University College at Buffalo

INTRODUCTION

This books is designed to present the reader with some very basic and practical writing techniques that are effective and simplistic. As with any process, there are rudiments that need to be mastered and principles to be learned so that the beginning writer may develop the necessary skills to be effective. Most textbooks written to address the subject of writing tend to be filled with complex instructions, rules, and principles, and generally serve to confuse rather than instruct. This book is composed in a straight-forward style that is neither formalistic nor too simplistic, but just right for anyone who wishes to learn how to write in a practical and effective manner with a minimum of effort.

THE FOUR BASIC PRINCIPLES OF EFFECTIVE WRITING

The four basic principles that constitute good writing are:

Purpose

Substance

Structure

Style.

Generally, all professional writers will agree that it is essential to understand these principles if one is to learn effective writing techniques.

PURPOSE

Purpose is defined as the writer's reason for writing a particular piece. All too often, a beginning writer will start an essay without a definite purpose clearly established in his mind. Such a start eventually causes the writer some confusion. He usually becomes lost during the writing and does not know exactly how to proceed. Having a clearly affixed purpose in mind serves to guide the writer at those moments of indecision. A person may go shopping for example, with a specific item in mind such as a jacket or an umbrella. He may become momentarily distracted by some other item of interest, and purchase the new article rather than the original one. This in turn might cause him to spend all his money, consequently, leaving him unable to purchase the item that he had originally started out to buy. The shopper with a clearly affixed purpose in mind may also become momentarily distracted by some other article of interest. He will, however, in direct contrast to a shopper without a definite purpose, most likely continue on and buy the original item because he has a clearly fixed purpose in mind.

Writing with a purpose works much the same way. A practical writer usually wants to achieve some sort of a goal. His purpose may be to explain a given subject or to convince the reader to pursue a specific course of action. When writing effectively, a practical writer should always consider the main purpose and then develop ideas and terms accordingly.

Purpose is the most important of the basic principles.

SUBSTANCE

Substance, sometimes called content, is defined as the material a writer puts into his work. If, for example, a baker wishes to bake a chocolate cake, he logically should include chocolate along with the other ingredients that constitute the recipe for that particular cake. Should he forget to include chocolate, it is obvious that he will not have a chocolate cake as he had originally planned, but a plain cake instead. Substance in writing is used much the same way. A writer must be sure to include all the content material that will ensure achievement of purpose. Just like making a cake, writing can be too rich or too plain. The practical writer will always strive to find the perfect blend to suit both the purpose of the piece and the taste of his audience.

STRUCTURE

Structure is defined as the way in which a written piece is put together. The relationships the writer establishes between various parts of the work are used to determine the overall structure of the piece. The general structure is also employed to define the work in terms of meaning and intent. When building a house, for example, it is generally wise to start at the foundation and build up, leaving the roof until last. The framework of the written work must be built upon a solid foundation and be logical in relationships if the writer wishes to convey meaning convincingly.

An example of the importance of structure can be seen through the use of symbols. The symbol "O" can stand for several things. It may represent a circle, a zero, or the letter O. What the "O" may represent is dependent upon the writer's purpose, and it can be easily defined through structure. If the writer wishes to communicate the specific idea of movement, he needs only to place the symbol "G" in front of the symbol "O", and then both clearly become letters used to communicate the idea of "to go." Should the writer add the symbol "D" to the end of the arrangement, then a new conceptual structure of GOD as a supreme being is defined. Should the writer rearrange that particular structure by moving the letters into a new structural relationships such as DOG, then yet another somewhat obvious meaning is conveyed.

Structure should always be used in relationship to purpose, and arranged so the writer can communicate ideas simply and effectively.

STYLE

Style is defined as the writer's choice of words and their respective arrangements. It is best understood in terms of the selection of ideas in relation to language. A punker, for example, is usually defined as a young person who chooses to color his hair orange or jet black, wear black leather clothes, and adorn himself with safety pins through various parts of his body. He can be said to have a particular style that identifies him as a punker. What if, however, a punker wishes to be employed in a bank? The general expectation of most people is that a bank employee is neat and business-like. Indeed, it is most probable that a customer would be reluctant to entrust his money to a person with orange hair and a black leather jacket who might say something like, "Wow—this is really neat man—look at all this bread!" If the punker really wishes to work in a bank, it is most likely that he will have to conform to all the expectations that people have regarding bank employees. He will probably have to get a haircut, wear a suit and tie, and speak in formal language such as "Good morning sir, may I be of service?"

Style, in terms of practical writing, ought to be used by the writer in order to be flexible. It should be related to the intended purpose of the writer, and be employed to conform to the general expectations of the audience.

RECAP

A good writer who wishes to be a strong communicator should always endeavor to keep the four basic principles in mind when writing to his audience. It is important to remember that:

> **Purpose**
>> **Substance**
>>> **Structure**
>>>> **Style**

are the four basic principles of practical and effective writing.

THE FOUR PRIMARY MODES

There are several different modes, also called techniques, of writing that professional writers use to make up what is known as good composition. Among those various modes, the four primary forms that ought to be part of every written piece are:

Exposition

Narration

Description

Argument/Persuasion.

EXPOSITION

Definition:

Exposition is that type of writing a writer uses to define, explain, interpret, and expose to his audience new forms of thought for consideration. Expository writing is used for the foundation of essays, research papers, newspaper and magazine articles, novels, movie scripts, reviews, and almost any other form of written discourse. The writer's purpose for employing exposition is to make the subject comprehensible and to *expose information* to the reader. Exposition ought to be well planned with a *logical structure* that the writer employs to exhibit a sense of progression. *Clarity* and coherence are necessary for the development of reader *interest*.

Method:

One of the surest ways to achieve clarity when using exposition is to arrange the material in a form that is best suited to the substance of the essay, to the writer's purpose, and to the needs of the reading audience. The writer may employ classification, time order, space order, analogy or contrast, deduction or induction, to name only a few, as methods of arranging material in such a way so that he can explain his message clearly and logically. Definition, example, metaphor, comparison and contrast, cause and effect, testimony, and analysis are also constituent parts of good exposition. Just as time is the basis of narration, and sensation the essence of description, likewise, clarity and logic are the cornerstones of effective expository writing.

The broader category of exposition as a mode, when employed properly, can be thought of as a combination of many rhetorical strategies which are used to clarify the writer's purpose, present information through exposure, and create a sense of heightened interest for the reader.

Major Points:

- Expose Information
- Clarity and Logic
- Interest

NARRATION

Definition:

Narration is a way of telling what happened. The purpose of using narration is to tell a story or relate an event. The key idea of narration is to *relate*. The most elementary form of narration is used to relate a series of *events* or experiences, in or out of *time sequences*. As a mode, narration is used to increase clarity and to hold the reader's interest. A professional writer employs narration as a method of development to illustrate and explain ideas. Most often, he uses narration to describe experiences or events that have some unusual significance for both the writer and the reader. The writer usually wishes to explain how he learned, through the experiences or events, a lesson of value from which the reader may also profit.

As a rhetorical strategy, narration is used to simply relate a story. The story must have a dominant theme or a *controlling idea* that is indicative of the writer's reason for telling the tale.

Method:

Effective narration in practical writing should be carefully organized. Since a narrative is used to describe events, its organization ought to be governed by some form of time order. Often, a writer will tell about a series of events in the exact order that they took place. This process is called chronological order, and insures that the time and sequence of the events will be logical.

Sometimes, however, a writer might find it useful to place events in an inverted manner by using flashbacks or time arrangements out of sequence. The use of this method permits the writer to give particular emphasis to important points while still adhering to logical order. The writer may start, for example, at the end of the narrative or in the middle, and then work his way back to the beginning of the story. This can add emphasis to the controlling idea. An important point to remember when using out of sequence narrative is that the reader must be able to follow the logic of the time order and the events. Following that rule will insure that the reader will neither be confused nor unclear about what happened.

It is wise to remember that to narrate means to tell a story in such a way as to relate events by linking them together, thus forging some type of a time chain. By arranging events in a form of orderly progression it is easier to illuminate the stages that lead to a specific result. Keep in mind that narrative is not real time. One incident may fill several pages, even though it only took seconds to occur. Conversely, an event that may have occurred over a period of several days may be explained through narration in a single paragraph or just a few sentences. For example, a war veteran might want to narrate the experience of a pitched moment in battle in order to demonstrate how his valor served unexpectedly to save his life. He might wish to describe a slow-motion account of the brief encounter by utilizing specific dialogue, depicting the setting in *detail,* and by providing a moment-to-moment account of his emotions. The writer may wish to compress time and events in the narrative in order to play down their significance, while simultaneously expanding time and other incidents so as to vividly heighten their impact. All this is known as duration, and designed to capture the reader's interest while making a specific point.

The writer's main point, when advanced through narration, can be used to influence the events covered and their arrangement. A straight chronological order is easy for the reader to follow and simple for the writer to manage because he employs it to relate events in the order of their actual occurrence. This method is particularly useful for a short narrative where the writer builds the story up logically to the last climactic event. The inverted method of narrative writing is a bit more complex to manage, and often needs *transitions* to signal relationships. Transitional expressions such as *afterwards* or *earlier* are employed to signal an order of events. Others such as *all day long* or *for an hour* are utilized to draw attention to the duration of events. Expressions such as *a week later* or *the next morning* are used to demonstrate the amount of time passed between events. The important aspect of transitions is that they are employed by a writer to serve the dual purpose of keeping the reader tracked to a time frame while simultaneously linking sentences and paragraphs in an efficient and smooth flowing manner.

The writer's use of *point of view* is also important in the narrative process. The writer ought to establish a consistent point of view that is relative to events. This fixes the writer's position in relation to situations and incidents in the story, and makes it easier for the reader to follow along during the narration. Point of view can best be conveyed through the use of *pronouns* such as the first–person, *I*, if the writer wishes to appear as a direct participant, and the third–person, *he, she, it,* and *they*, if the writer wishes to appear as an observer or reporter. The writer's relation in time sequences can best be conveyed by *verb tense*. By combining the first–person pronoun with the present tense, the writer can create a sense of immediacy and subjectivity. To create distance and objectivity, the writer can combine third–person pronouns with the past tense. This can be shown by comparing and contrasting the present tense example of ". . . I see the enemy coming at me with fixed bayonets!" to the past tense example of " . . . he saw the enemy coming at him with fixed bayonets!" There are many choices available to the writer, and they all are dependent upon his actual involvement in the narrative and his purpose for writing the story. Two points to bear in mind when using pronouns and verb tenses are as follows:

(1) the chosen person, whether first or third, ought to be consistent throughout the story;

(2) the verb tense should not be shifted unnecessarily from present to past, past to present, or present to future.

Major Points:

- Related Events
- Time Sequence
- Controlling Idea
- Details
- Transitions
- Point of View

SALVATION

Langston Hughes

*Born in Joplin, Missouri, Langston Hughes (1902–1967),
is an important figure in the Harlem Renaissance whose
poetry, fiction, and plays have contributed greatly to
American literature. Known as a writer who developed his
skills during the Harlem Renaissance, Hughes is perhaps
best known for his* The Weary Blues *(1926) and other
books of poetry that express racial pride, African-American
tradition, and a knowledge of jazz. This selection is taken
from his autobiography* The Big Sea *(1940).*

I was saved from sin when I was going on thirteen. But not
really saved. It happened like this. There was a big revival at
my Auntie Reed's church. Every night for weeks there had
been much preaching, singing, praying, and shouting, and
some very hardened sinners had been brought to Christ, and
the membership of the church had grown by leaps and
bounds. Then just before the revival ended, they held a special
meeting for children, "to bring the young lambs to the fold."
My aunt spoke of it for days ahead. That night, I was escorted
to the front row and placed on the mourners' bench with all
other young sinners, who had not yet been brought to Jesus.

My aunt told me that when you were saved you saw a
light, and something happened to you inside! And Jesus came
into your life! And God was with you from then on! She said
you could see and hear and feel Jesus in your soul. I believed
her. I have heard a great many old people say the same thing
and it seemed to me they ought to know. So I sat there calmly
in the hot, crowded church, waiting for Jesus to come to me.

The preacher preached a wonderful rhythmical sermon,
all moans and shouts and lonely cries and dire pictures of hell,
and then he sang a song about the ninety and nine safe in the
fold, but one little lamb was left out in the cold. Then he said:
"Won't you come? Won't you come to Jesus? Young lambs,
won't you come?" And he held out his arms to all us young
sinners there on the mourners' bench. And the little girls

cried. And some of them jumped up and went to Jesus right away. But most of us just sat there. A great many old people came and knelt around us and prayed, old women with jet-black faces and braided hair, old men with work-gnarled hands. And the church sang a song about the lower lights are burning, some poor sinners to be saved. And the whole building rocked with prayer and song.

Still I kept waiting to *see* Jesus.

Finally all the young people had gone to the altar and were saved, but one boy and me. He was a rounder's son named Westley. Westley and I were surrounded by sisters and deacons praying. It was very hot in the church, and getting late now. Finally Westley said to me in a whisper: "God damn! I'm tired o' sitting here. Let's get up and be saved." So he got up and was saved.

Then I was left all alone on the mourners' bench. My aunt came and knelt at my knees and cried, while prayers and songs swirled all around me in the little church. The whole congregation prayed for me alone, in a mightily wail of moans and voices. And I kept waiting serenely for Jesus, waiting, waiting—but he didn't come. I wanted to see him, but nothing happened to me. Nothing! I wanted something to happen to me, but nothing happened.

I heard the songs and the minister saying: "Why don't you come? My dear child, why don't you come to Jesus? Jesus is waiting for you. He wants you. Why don't you come? Sister Reed, what is this child's name?"

"Langston," my aunt sobbed.

"Langston, why don't you come? Why don't you come and be saved? Oh, Lamb of God! Why don't you come?"

Now it was really getting late. I began to be ashamed of myself, holding everything up so long. I began to wonder what God thought about Westley, who certainly hadn't seen Jesus either, but who was now sitting proudly on the platform, swinging his knickerbockered legs and grinning down at me, surrounded by deacons and old women on their knees praying. God had not struck Westley dead for taking his name in vain or for lying in the temple. So I decided that maybe to save further trouble, I'd better lie, too, and say that Jesus had come, and get up and be saved.

13

So I got up.

Suddenly the whole room broke into a sea of shouting, as they saw me rise. Waves of rejoicing swept the place. Women leaped in the air. My aunt threw her arms around me. The minister took me by the hand and led me to the platform.

When things quieted down, in a hushed silence, punctuated by a few ecstatic "Amens," all the new young lambs were blessed in the name of God. Then joyous singing filled the room.

That night, for the last time in my life but one—for I was a big boy twelve years old—I cried. I cried, in bed alone, and couldn't stop. I buried my head under the quilts, but my aunt heard me. She woke up and told my uncle I was crying because the Holy Ghost had come into my life, and because I had seen Jesus. But I was really crying because I couldn't bear to tell her that I had lied, that I had deceived everybody in the church, that I hadn't seen Jesus, and that now I didn't believe there was a Jesus any more, since he didn't come to help me.

Langston Hughes. "Salvation." *The Compact Reader*, Second Edition. Jane E. Aaron, Editor. St. Martin's Press, 1987, pp. 64–66. ISBN: 0-312-15308-2.

Suggestions for discussion and writing:

1. Compare Hughes' "Salvation" to Rothchild's "Melting-Pot High." What purpose does each author have in mind?
2. How is description used in narration?
3. Does Hughes tell his story in flashbacks or straight chronological order?
4. Write a narrative in which you present two versions of an actual event. One version should be related the way you wished it to occur, and the other version should be recounted the way it actually happened.
5. Think of an ethnic experience that had a profound impact upon your memory. List the sequence of events that led up to the experience, and then draft a narrative relating those events.

THE DISCOVERY OF COCA-COLA

E.J. Kahn, Jr.

E. J. Kahn, Jr. is the author of a book entitled The Big Drink, *and has served as a writer for* The New Yorker *magazine for over forty years. Specializing in the American scene, Kahn has written about America at War, Harvard, Burlesque, Frank Sinatra, and the invention of Coca-Cola. He relates the invention of the popular soda first as a medicine and then as the discovery that led to its becoming a soft drink.*

The man who invented Coca-Cola was not a native Atlantan, but on the day of his funeral every drugstore in town testimonially shut up shop. He was John Styth Pemberton, born 1833 in Knoxville, Georgia, eighty miles away. Sometimes known as Doctor, Pemberton was a pharmacist who, during the Civil War, led a cavalry troop under General Joe Wheeler. He settled in Atlanta in 1869, and soon began brewing such patent medicines as Triplex Liver Pills and Globe of Flower Cough Syrup. In 1885, he registered a trademark for something called French Wine Coca—Ideal Nerve and Tonic Stimulant; a few months later he formed the Pemberton Chemical Company, and recruited the services of a bookkeeper named Frank M. Robinson, who not only had a good head for figures but, attached to it, so exceptional a nose that he could audit the composition of a batch of syrup merely by sniffing it. In 1886, a year in which, as contemporary Coca-Cola officials like to point out, Conan Doyle unveiled Sherlock Holmes and France unveiled the Statue of Liberty— Pemberton unveiled a syrup that he called Coca-Cola. It was a modification of his French Wine Coca. He had taken out the wine and added a pinch of caffeine, and, when the end product tasted awful, had thrown in some extract of cola (or kola) nut and a few other oils, blending the mixture in a three-legged iron pot in his back yard and swishing it around with an oar. He distributed it to soda fountains in used beer bottles, and Robinson, with his flowing bookkeeper's script, presently

15

devised a label, on which "Coca-Cola" was written in the fashion that is still employed. Pemberton looked upon his concoction less as a refreshment than as a headache cure, especially for people whose throbbing temples could be traced to overindulgence. On a morning late in 1886, one such victim of the night before dragged himself into an Atlanta drugstore and asked for a dollop of Coca-Cola. Druggists customarily stirred a teaspoonful of syrup into a glass of water, but in this instance the factotum on duty was too lazy to walk to the fresh-water tap, a couple of feet off. Instead, he mixed the syrup with some charged water, which was closer at hand. The suffering customer perked up almost at once, and word quickly spread that the best Coca-Cola was a fizzy one.

Kahn, E.J. Jr. "The Discovery of Coca-Cola." *Patterns Plus*, Third Edition. Mary Lou Conlin, Editor. Houghton Mifflin Company, 1990, pp. 21–22. ISBN 0-395-51691-9.

Suggestions for discussion and writing:

1. What is the writer's point of view?
2. Why does the author use antiquated words in the story?
3. Write a brief first-person narrative relating something you did.
4. Write a short narrative in which you describe a significant discovery that you made.
5. Write a long descriptive narrative using either a dark or light tone to set a mood.

MELTING-POT HIGH

John Rothchild

John Rothchild is a journalist and an essayist. He has worked for The St. Petersburg Times, The New York Times, *and* The Washington Post. *A Harvard graduate, Rothchild is a world traveler who has published five books and numerous articles which have been published in magazines such as* Esquire, Harper's, *and* Rolling Stone *to name only a few. His essay "Melting-Pot High" is a narration of the history of the largest high school in Miami, Florida, and a discussion of diversity. It first appeared in the June 1985* Esquire *magazine special issue about "The Soul of America."*

In a single summer the Mariel boatlift delivered a mass of newcomers to Miami's shores equal to nearly one-third of the city's entire population. Haitians still wade in from scuttled and unseaworthy vessels, Colombians fly in, Nicaraguans drive in via Mexico to escape their left-wing government. Two decades ago there were Cuban airlifts, and a decade before that the Bronx and Chicago carlifts brought a steady supply of Yankees escaping cold weather.

Over the past thirty years Miami has absorbed more immigrants per capita than any other American city. Miami is two hundred years of New England compressed into fifty: people hardly settle down long enough to learn about mildew and hurricanes before they are thought of as forefathers by more recent arrivals, who themselves are rendered obsolete in a boatlift or two. Huge incursions make foreigners of the erstwhile natives. Erstwhile natives either migrate up to Fort Lauderdale or stay and speculate: When will all these outsiders ever fit in?

Just off Flagler Street and a few blocks from downtown sits the oldest high school in the city, Miami Senior High School. An ornate structure built in the old Spanish style, Miami High looks as though it were destined for Spanish occupation: less a public school than an old San Juan hotel or a cloister from the Christianized Moors. It has archways as deep as tunnels, corridors of brown Cuban tile as wide as skating rinks, restful little indoor patios with potted palms, a big bust of the great Cuban poet Jose Martí, and lately a student body that can recognize him.

The students break for lunch across Colombia Park, Burger King to the right of them and the Cafeteria Mirita, with its *medianoche* sandwiches and *pastelitos*, to the left: 90 percent of them Hispanic; 6 percent black; the previous Miami establishment winnowed to 4 percent "other"—yesterday's gringo ruling class officially dismissed as non-Hispanic white.

Gringo alumni can trace their influence back as far as Prohibition, when the new Miami High School opened its doors to the children of immigrants arriving on Henry Flagler's trainlifts from Georgia or North Carolina. Miami was still *Miamuh*. The school nickname, Stingaree, was the likely local pronunciation of *stingray*; the yearbooks were edited by the Prossers, Kents, Wrights, and Lassiters of this world. William Jennings Bryan, the silver-tongued lot salesman in Coral Gables, was their favorite guest speaker. Did they foresee the inevitable even then? In the school's debating club the most popular topic in the early 1920s was: "Resolved that all immigration should be prohibited for the present."

The occasional Cuban student complemented the Miami High architecture: Bebe Rebozo, for instance, and Desi Arnaz. The Arnaz family had fled to Miami after the fall of Cuban president Gerardo Machado in the 1930s. There weren't enough Cubans at Miami High to be thought of categorically, and perhaps that was a key to their acceptance. For thirty years in the city's Anglolithic Era the blacks were corralled into two tight little ghettos and attended separate schools, and the anti-Semitic hoteliers working for developer Carl Fisher on Miami Beach looked out for "Jewish noses." Miami High had its Courtesy Week, its Father and Son Banquets, and the only real threats to cultural stability were the incoming Yankees.

What divided Stingarees then was North versus South, although in those days there was no official recognition of it— registrars didn't have categories like non-Confederate white. Billie Wills, one of those unforgettable teachers who make high schools worthwhile, got a job in the Miami High Spanish department in 1957, when it was still Yankee, not Spanish accents that disturbed the locals. She remembers the lunchroom, generally the place where such differences sort themselves out: "Southerners wouldn't sit with northern people. I was of Greek descent, but it wasn't fashionable to advertise it. One of our history teachers wouldn't sit near me because one of my cake recipes called for alcohol."

More important than any of this was Stingaree pride. By the 1940s Miami High had produced Florida senator George Smathers, tennis star Gardnar Mulloy, Phil Graham of *The Washington Post*, Arnold Tucker of the Army backfield, judges and legislators too numerous to mention, regional and national football championships, and Veronica Lake. More crucial in that era than any Civil War was the annual game with rival Edison High School (Edison never won).

High school spirit turns out to be one of the hidden safeguards of democracy, uniting the upcoming generations around arbitrary distinctions like Stings versus Red Raiders, as opposed to something serious.

The 1950s brought thousands of easterners, many of them Jewish, to the Miami area. The Jews had broken out of their vacationers' ghetto on South Beach; hoteliers in other sections repealed their anti-Semitic prohibitions. There were more Jewish lawyers, doctors, entrepreneurs throughout the region, and enough Jewish students at Miami High to raise the question: But will these outsiders ever fit in?

Across from Miami High was Shirley's, a hamburger place known as the Christian hangout. The Mason-Dixon line in the school cafeteria gave way to more up-to-date distinctions as Christians on both sides of the southern question closed ranks. Old grads from this period can't wait to ask: "Have you heard about 'Little Jerusalem'?" Little Jerusalem was the school's east courtyard, informally adopted as the spot where Jews would naturally want to congregate.

School social clubs, sponsored by local civic organizations, continued to pick their little magnolia blossoms right out of the classrooms. For decades this was Miami's way of reinforcing the caste system of society at large against the threat of too much commingling in the schools. If you ever doubted where you really belonged, the social clubs inevitably sorted it all out. To be tapped for Little Women or Honoria was one thing; to be Jewish was another. Jewish students countered by joining the more liberal-minded social clubs: Anchor and the Junior Debs.

More important than any of this was being a Stingaree. From the yearbooks, you can almost write a Law of Inevitable Acceptance: Goldfarbs and Leibowitzes first appearing as mere faces, then as honored scholars; as pep boosters; as academic-club members; as occasional Honorias or Little Women; and at last as homecoming royalty—the relentless straight line of Miami High goyishe kings and queens broken by Joan Ackerman in 1963.

About the time of this Judaic ascension to royalty, Batista fell, and suddenly Little Jerusalem ceased to exist at all. The Cuban Revolution indirectly wiped it out. Suddenly there was a Judeo-Yankee-southern establishment, as opposed to the Cubans who were installed on the fourth floor of the high school. Billie Wills' students finally had somebody Spanish to talk to, and so, as the teachers remember it, "the interest in Spanish was beginning to drop." There were the Prossers and Wrights of this world, not to mention the Goldfarbs and Leibowitzes, abandoning the Spanish Club for the French club, Entre Nous, hoping to put distance between themselves and the living Hispanics, who wore strange blazers with the names of their prep schools back in Havana.

Miami as a whole was going through it, measuring its limited compassion for victims of communism against its skepticism of Caribbean intruders. Many of the first Cubans were sons and daughters of professors, government officials, and industrialists. They distinguished themselves in the Miami High classrooms as the Jews once had. Taking weekend rifle practice with paramilitary units in the Everglades added to their dramatic appeal.

Still, to be Little Women or Honorias was not to be Cuban. A separate but equal Pan American Club was devised in 1963 by Diego Garcia, a teacher with Spanish parents. Billie Wills, who had stopped teaching languages altogether since the exodus to French, devoted herself to the challenge of Cuban adjustment as the school's activities director.

Wills remembers the Cubans coming off the fourth floor to read speeches and leave flowers at the statue of José Martí, their national hero, who previously was just a bust on the

20

lawn. Martí was donated to Miami High after the school's Million Dollar Band took a trip to Havana in the 1940s, back when our interest in Latin America was not so reciprocal.

"I felt for those kids," Wills says. "One time they staged a big Cuban party, or *cumparsa*. Their mothers made all the costumes. Incredible costumes. Cubans from all over the country, dignitaries, politicians, came to see the show. They wanted to prove how great they were, and they did."

By the time Miami High was integrated in 1970, the blacks had to wonder if they weren't being bused into Caracas or Santiago. In 1971 there were Bill Capps and Nancy Arnold, token gringos in the homecoming court; on the first pages of that year's yearbook are six Alvarezes and six Acostas. History and science were being taught through bilingual instruction for students with language difficulties. The Prossers and Wrights of this world were vanishing toward the 4-percent level of the present. Administrator Pete Nelson walks through the wide corridors today and jokes, "I'd be hard pressed to show you one."

Billie Wills, who began her career teaching Spanish to the English, has switched to teaching English to the Spanish. Diego Garcia, the former Spanish teacher and founder of the Pan American Club, is the current Miami High principal. Spanish is the language of the hallways; English is the language of the classroom. Non-Hispanic blacks are frightfully outnumbered and practice -*ar*, -*er*, and -*ir* verbs in the hope of landing local counter jobs.

Billie Wills had the challenge of helping the immigrants from the 1980 Mariel boatlift, along with the Nicaraguans, to adjust. Some were named Fidelito and Raulito, raised on communism, speaking in strange and disturbing phrases foreign to normal Miami-domestic Spanish. Wills remembers the first Marielito year as follows: "They came in droves. You'd say, 'Sit down,' and they'd say '¿*Que*?' This was America, Land of Freedom. Freedom meant you didn't have to sit down. Some stood on chairs during classes. The toughest ones dropped out."

You can see it in the yearbooks of the early 1980s. Marielitos appearing first as photos, then as class officers, and finally in 1984 there is a Marielito student-government president. No king or queen yet, but it is inevitable.

In 1984 a video class is making a tape about fatal mistakes in syntax that result from too-literal translations between English and Spanish: little skits in which a lady unwittingly announces she is pregnant *(embarazada)* when she means she is embarrassed, or in which a man says he is *intoxicado* meaning "drunk," when *intoxicado* really means "poisoned." Billie Wills is teaching the class; the students are mostly from Mariel. She asks whether their Cuban relatives will be coming if they get the chance, and all but one raises his hand.

Miami High is the essence of Miami's present and perpetual condition: the outsiders taking over, the erstwhile natives estranged.

And yet, is there not something reassuringly familiar here? The second floor is called the Marielito floor; more seasoned immigrants occupy the third and the first. The important distinctions are early Cuban versus late Cuban, Nicaraguan versus Colombian. The Cuban establishment wonders of these late arrivals: Will they ever fit in?

More important than any of this is Stingaree pride. The 1983 Miami High yearbook speculates:

"Where else but at Miami High School would the 89.2 percent Hispanic population, a minority, be a majority to the 10 percent Caucasians who in time learned to eat pastelitos and say 'ah, chico' like most of the crowd?

". . . But as he became part of the institution, he learned that before he was a Cuban, black, or white, he was a Stingaree, and that was all that really mattered."

Rothchild, John. "Melting-Pot High." *The Compact Reader*, Second Edition, 1987. Jane E. Aaron, Editor, pp. 78–83. ISBN: 0-312-15308-2.

Suggestions for discussion and writing:

1. Which events does Rothchild explain?

2. How does Rothchild arrange time chronologically?

3. Is the high school a representation of the United States?

4. Write a narrative essay in which you relate an experience when you felt like an outsider.

5. Write a narrative essay discussing why sports fans of various cities identify the local football or baseball team as "our guys."

DESCRIPTION

Definition:

Description, in terms of writing, is used to tell how something looks, tastes, smells, sounds, feels, and acts. When employing description the writer deals with things, people, places, scenes, animals, moods, and impressions. He, in effect, makes the content of the writing sensuous. The two primary purposes for using description are to portray a *sense impression* and to *indicate a mood*. Description, as a mode, is used to help a writer create an impression or a mood that is vivid for the reader. It is important for the writer to understand that description is not an independent mode, and that it ought to be used in conjunction with some other mode of writing, preferably narration, if it is to be employed effectively. Good descriptive writing is best used in short passages as an aid for explaining or narrating something.

Method:

Descriptive writing ought to be employed to create a single dominant impression. The writer should include only those *details* that can be used to contribute to that impression. Some writers believe that good written description should be flowery, poetic, and filled with ornate figures of speech. To the contrary, it is better for a writer to be simplistic in his writing and to include only those words and details necessary as he tries to create the dominant impression.

To produce effective description it is necessary for the writer to bring things or events into a sharper *focus* for the benefit of the reader. The focus is usually on a *quality* or a *detail* of what is being described, such as "the cooling rain" or "the teacher with a *frayed* shirt collar." Focus can also be produced through comparisons such as "the rain drummed on the roof *like* metal pellets hitting a tile floor." *Qualities* are usually indicated by the use of *adnouns (adjectives)*, *details* by *noun phrases* and sometimes *adnouns (adjectives)*, and *comparisons* by *similes* and *metaphors*. A field of wild flowers might be described metaphorically as "a sea of green water sprayed with tiny white flecks." A good example of the use of simile

23

might be "the flowers seemed to glow like greenish fluorescent fireflies on a dark night." These techniques can be utilized so that the writer creates both a dominant impression and continuity of the principal theme.

Again, *point of view* is important because of the writer's *psychological* and *physical* relation to the subject. When a writer wants to lessen the distance between the writer and the reader, and better communicate the writer's feelings and biases as part of the message, he uses subjective description by employing first and second-person pronouns such as *I* and *you*. Conversely, the writer uses *objective* description by employing third-person pronouns such as *he* and *they* in order to place a greater distance between himself and the subject.

Like narrative writing, descriptive writing emanates from the writer's powers of observation. However, where narrative writing is used to recount events and experiences in time, descriptive writing is employed to evoke the sensory aspects of sight, sound, and the sense of those events and experiences. The two modes are complimentary and usually employed in tandem.

Major Points:
- Senses and Impressions
- Indicate Moods
- Focus
- Qualities and Details
- Point of View

ON ABRAHAM LINCOLN

Nathaniel Hawthorne

Nathaniel Hawthorne (1804–1864), one of America's great writers of fiction, is best known for his novels The House of the Seven Gables *and* The Scarlet Letter. *He exerted a great influence over American literature through his many books and short stories dealing with the problems of guilt, good, and evil.*

Unquestionably, Western man though he be, and Kentuckian by birth, President Lincoln is the essential representative of all Yankees, and the veritable specimen, physically, of what the world seems determined to regard as our characteristic qualities. It is the strangest and yet the fittest thing in the jumble of human vicissitudes, that he, out of so many millions, unlooked for, unselected by any intelligible process that could be based upon his genuine qualities, unknown to those who chose him, and unsuspected of what endowments may adapt him for his tremendous responsibility, should have found the way open for him to fling his lank personality into the chair of state—where, I presume, it was his first impulse to throw his legs on the council-table, and tell the Cabinet Ministers a story. There is no describing his lengthy awkwardness, nor the uncouthness of his movement; and yet it seemed as if I had been in the habit of seeing him daily, and had shaken hands with him a thousand times in some village street; so true was he to the aspect of the pattern American, though with a certain extravagance which, possibly, I exaggerated still further by the delighted eagerness with which I took it in. If put to guess his calling and livelihood, I should have taken him for a country school-master as soon as anything else. He was dressed in a rusty black frock coat and pantaloons, unbrushed, and worn so faithfully that the suit had adapted itself to the curves and angularities of his figure, and had grown to be an outer skin of the man. His hair was black, still unmixed with gray, stiff, somewhat bushy, and had apparently been acquainted with neither brush nor comb that morning, after the disarrangement of the pillow; and as to a nightcap, Uncle Abe probably knows nothing of such effeminacies. His complexion is dark and sallow, betokening, I fear, an insalubrious atmosphere around the White House; he has thick black eyebrows and an impending brow; his nose is large, and the lines about his mouth are very strongly defined.

The whole physiognomy is as coarse a one as you would meet anywhere in the length and breadth of the States; but, withal, it is redeemed, illuminated, softened, and brightened by a kindly though serious look out of his eyes, and an expression of homely sagacity, that seems weighted with rich results of village experience. A great deal of native sense; no bookish cultivation, no refinement; honest at heart, and thoroughly so, and yet, in some sort, sly—at least, endowed with a sort of tact and wisdom that are akin to craft, and would impel him, I think, to take an antagonist in flank, rather than to make a bull-run at him right in front. But, on the whole, I like this sallow, queer, sagacious visage, with the homely human sympathies that warmed it; and, for my small share in the matter, would as lief have Uncle Abe for a ruler as any man whom it would have been practicable to put in his place.

Hawthorne, Nathaniel. "On Abraham Lincoln." *Thinking in Writing*, Second Edition. Donald McQuade and Robert Atwan, Editors. Alfred A. Knopf, 1983, p. 286. ISBN: 0-394-32819-1.

ON ABRAHAM LINCOLN

Edward Dicey

*Edward Dicey (1832–1911) was a noted English journalist
and writer specializing in foreign affairs. He worked for the*
Daily Telegraph, *and served as editor of the* Observer.
*Dicey exercised considerable influence over public opinion,
and was particularly good at descriptive writing which
accounted for his popularity in England.*

———————————

Personally, his aspect is one which, once seen, cannot easily be
forgotten. If you take the stock English caricature of the typi-
cal Yankee, you have the likeness of the President. To say that
he is ugly is nothing: to add that his figure is grotesque is to
convey no adequate impression. Fancy a man six-foot high,
and thin *out of* proportion, with long bony arms and legs,
which, somehow, seem to be always in the way, with large
rugged hands, which grasp you like a vice when shaking
yours, with a long scraggy neck, and a chest too narrow for
the great arms hanging by its side; add to this figure, a head
cocoa-nut shaped and somewhat too small for such a stature,
covered with rough, uncombed and uncombable lank dark
hair, that stands out in every direction at once; a face fur-
rowed, wrinkled, and indented, as though it had been scarred
by vitriol; a high narrow forehead; and, sunk deep beneath
bushy eyebrows, two bright, somewhat dreamy eyes, that
seemed to gaze through you without looking at you; a few
irregular blotches of black bristly hair in the place where
beard and whiskers ought to grow; a close-set, thin-lipped,
stern mouth, with two rows of large white teeth; and a nose
and ears, which have been taken by mistake from a head of
twice the size. Clothe this figure, then, in a long, tight, badly-
fitting suit of black, creased, soiled, and puckered up at every
salient point of the figure and every point of this figure is
salient—put on large, ill-fitting boots, gloves too long for the
long bony fingers, and a fluffy hat, covered to the top with
dusty, puffy crape; and then add to all this an air of strength,
physical as well as moral, and a strange look of dignity

27

coupled with all this grotesqueness, and you will have the impression left upon me by Abraham Lincoln. You would never say he was a gentleman: you would still less say he was not one. There are some women about whom no one ever thinks in connexion with beauty, one way or the other—and there are men to whom the epithet of "gentlemanlike" or "ungentlemanlike" appears utterly incongruous, and of such the President is one. Still there is about him a complete absence of pretension, and an evident desire to be courteous to everybody, which is the essence, if not the outward form, of high-breeding. There is a softness, too, about his smile, and a sparkle of dry humour about his eye which redeem the expression on his face. . . .

Dicey, Edward. "On Abraham Lincoln." *Thinking in Writing,* Second Edition. Donald McQuade and Robert Atwan, Editors. Alfred A. Knopf, 1983, pp. 286–288. ISBN: 0-394-32819-1.

Suggestions for discussions and writing:

1. Consider the word choice of each author and then discuss whether the terms are designed to be subjective or objective.

2. Discuss focus as a device in each essay.

3. Write an essay in which you examine the attitude of each writer toward Abraham Lincoln.

4. How is point of view presented in each of these articles?

5. Write an essay in which you describe the President of the United States.

THIS MAN HAS EXPIRED

Robert Johnson

Robert Johnson is a contemporary writer who wrote this particular piece for the Commonwealth Foundation in 1989. His work is a statement about the death penalty. It is sensitive, contemporary, and somewhat disturbing.

We entered the witness area, a room within the death chamber, and took our seats. A picture window covering the front wall of the witness room offered a clear view of the electric chair, which was about twelve feet away from us and well illuminated. The chair, a large, high-back solid oak structure with imposing black straps, dominated the death chamber. Behind it, on the back wall, was an open panel full of coils and lights. Peeling paint hung from the ceiling and walls; water stains from persistent leaks were everywhere in evidence.

Two officers, one a hulking figure weighing some 400 pounds, stood alongside the electric chair. Each had his hands crossed at the lap and wore a forbidding, blank expression on his face. The witnesses gazed at them and the chair, most of us scribbling notes furiously. We did this, I suppose, as much to record the experience as to have a distraction from the growing tension. A correctional officer entered the witness room and announced that a trial run of the machinery would be undertaken. Seconds later, lights flashed on the control panel behind the chair indicating that the chair was in working order. A white curtain, opened for the test, separated the chair and the witness area. After the test, the curtain was drawn. More tests were performed behind the curtain. Afterwards, the curtain was reopened, and would be left open until the execution was over. Then it would be closed to allow the officers to remove the body.

A handful of high-level correctional officers were present in the death chamber, standing just outside the witness area. There were two regional administrators, the director of the Department of Corrections, and the prison warden. The prisoner's chaplain and lawyer were also present. Other than the chaplain's black religious garb, subdued grey pinstripes and bland correctional uniforms prevailed. All parties were quite solemn.

At 10:58 the prisoner entered the death chamber. He was, I knew from my research, a man with a checkered, tragic past. He had been grossly abused as a child, and went on to become grossly abusive of others. I was told he could not describe his life, from childhood on, without talking about confrontations in defense of a precarious sense of self—at home, in school, on the streets, in the prison yard. Belittled by life and choking with rage, he was hungry to be noticed. Paradoxically, he had found his moment in the spotlight, but it was a dim and unflattering light cast before a small and unappreciative audience. "He'd pose for cameras in the chair—for the attention," his counselor had told me earlier in the day. But the truth was that the prisoner wasn't smiling, and there were no cameras.

The prisoner walked quickly and silently toward the chair, an escort of officers in tow. His eyes were turned downward, his expression a bit glazed. Like many before him, the prisoner had threatened to stage a last stand. But that was lifetimes ago, on death row. In the death house, he joined the humble bunch and kept to the executioner's schedule. He appeared to have given up on life before he died in the chair.

En route to the chair, the prisoner stumbled slightly, as if the momentum of the event had overtaken him. Were he not held securely by two officers, one at each elbow, he might have fallen. Were the routine to be broken in this or indeed any other way, the officers believe, the prisoner might faint or panic or become violent, and have to be forcibly placed in the chair. Perhaps as a precaution, when the prisoner reached the chair he did not turn on his own but rather was turned, firmly but without malice, by the officers in his escort. These included the two men at his elbows, and four others who followed behind him. Once the prisoner was seated, again with help, the officers strapped him into the chair.

The execution team worked with machine precision. Like a disciplined swarm, they enveloped him. Arms, legs, stomach, chest, and head were secured in a matter of seconds. Electrodes were attached to a cap holding his head and to the strap holding his exposed right leg. A leather mask was placed over his face. The last officer mopped the prisoner's brow, then touched his hand in a gesture of farewell.

During the brief procession to the electric chair, the prisoner was attended by a chaplain. As the execution team worked feverishly to secure the condemned man's body, the chaplain, who appeared to be upset, leaned over him and placed his forehead in contact with the prisoner's, whispering urgently. The priest might have been praying, but I had the impression he was consoling the man, perhaps assuring him that a forgiving God awaited him in the next life. If he heard the chaplain, I doubt the man comprehended his message. He didn't seem comforted. Rather, he looked stricken and appeared to be in shock. Perhaps the priest's urgent ministrations betrayed his doubts that the prisoner could hold himself together. The chaplain then withdrew at the warden's request, allowing the officers to affix the death mask.

The strapped and masked figure sat before us, utterly alone, waiting to be killed. The cap and mask dominated his face. The cap was nothing more than a sponge encased in a leather shell with a metal piece at the top to accent an electrode. It looked decrepit and resembled a cheap, ill-fitting toupee. The mask, made entirely of leather, appeared soiled and worn. It had two parts. The bottom part covered the chin and mouth, the top the eyes and lower forehead. Only the nose was exposed. The effect of the rigidly restrained body, together with the bizarre cap and the protruding nose, was nothing short of grotesque. A faceless man breathed before us in a tragicomic trance, waiting for a blast of electricity that would extinguish his life. Endless seconds passed. His last act was to swallow, nervously, pathetically, with his Adam's apple bobbing. I was struck by that simple movement then, and can't forget it even now. It told me, as nothing else did, that in the prisoner's restrained body, behind that mask, lurked a fellow human being who, at some level, however primitive, knew or sensed himself to be moments from death.

Johnson, Robert. "This Man Has Expired." *Patterns Plus*, Third Edition. Mary Lou Conlin, Editor. Houghton Mifflin Company, 1990, pp. 97–99. ISBN: 0-395-51691-9.

Suggestions for discussion and writing:

1. Why does Johnson use the term "We" to begin his article?
2. Discuss the subjective and objective aspects of the essay.
3. Does Johnson use focus in his article?
4. Write an essay in which you describe an unpleasant experience.
5. Put yourself in the prisoner's place and describe what you think you might feel under those circumstances.

ROCK OF AGES

Joan Didion

Joan Didion is a novelist and essayist well known for her power to command description. She has written four books, articles for Vogue, Life, *and* Esquire, *as well as screen plays such as* A Star Is Born *and* Panic in Needle Park. *This article is an excerpt from her book* Slouching Towards Bethlehem. *A graduate of the University of California at Berkeley, she has traveled extensively and brings an experienced journalistic eye for detail to her works.*

Alcatraz Island is covered with flowers now: orange and yellow nasturtiums, geraniums, sweet grass, blue iris, black-eyed Susans. Candytuft springs up through the cracked concrete in the exercise yard. Ice plant carpets the rusting catwalks. "WARNING! KEEP OFF! U.S. PROPERTY," the sign still reads, big and yellow and visible for perhaps a quarter of a mile, but since March 21,1963, the day they took the last thirty or so men off the island and sent them to prisons less expensive to maintain, the warning has been only *pro forma*, the gun turrets empty, the cell blocks abandoned. It is not an unpleasant place to be, out there on Alcatraz with only the flowers and the wind and a bell buoy moaning and the tide surging through the Golden Gate, but to like a place like that you have to want a moat.

I sometimes do, which is what I am talking about here. Three people live on Alcatraz Island now. John and Marie Hart live in the same apartment they had for the sixteen years that he was a prison guard; they raised five children on the island, back when their neighbors were the Birdman and Mickey Cohen, but the Birdman and Mickey Cohen are gone now and so are the Harts' children, moved away, the last married in a ceremony on the island in June 1966. One other person lives on Alcatraz, a retired merchant seaman named Bill Doherty, and, between them, John Hart and Bill Doherty are responsible to the General Services Administration for maintaining a twenty-four-hour watch over the twenty-two-acre island. John Hart has a dog named Duffy, and Bill Doherty has a dog named Duke, and although the dogs are primarily good company they are also the first line of defense on Alcatraz Island. Marie Hart has a corner window which looks out to the San Francisco skyline, across a mile and a half of bay, and she sits there and paints, "views" or plays her organ, songs like "Old Black Joe" and "Please Go 'Way and Let Me Sleep." Once a week the Harts take their boat to San Francisco to pick up their mail and shop at the big Safeway in the Marina, and occasionally Marie Hart gets off the island to visit her children. She likes to keep in touch with them by telephone, but for ten months recently, after a Japanese freighter cut the cable, there was no telephone service to or from Alcatraz. Every morning the KGO traffic reporter drops the San Francisco *Chronicle* from his helicopter, and when he has time he stops for coffee. No one else comes out there except a man from the General Services Administration named Thomas Scott, who brings out an occasional congressman or somebody who wants to buy the island or, once in a while, his wife and small son, for a picnic. Quite a few people would like to buy the island, and Mr. Scott reckons that it would bring about five million dollars in a sealed-bid auction, but the General Services Administration is powerless to sell it until Congress acts on a standing proposal to turn the island into a "peace park." Mr. Scott says that he will be glad to get Alcatraz off his hands, but the charge of a fortress island could not be something a man gives up without ambivalent thoughts.

I went out there with him a while ago. Any child could imagine a prison more like a prison than Alcatraz looks, for what bars and wires there are seem perfunctory, beside the point; the island itself was the prison, and the cold tide its wall. It is precisely what they called it: the Rock. Bill Doherty and Duke lowered the dock for us, and in the station wagon on the way up the cliff Bill Doherty told Mr. Scott about small repairs he had made or planned to make. Whatever repairs get made on Alcatraz are made to pass the time, a kind of caretaker's scrimshaw, because the government pays for no upkeep at all on the prison; in 1963 it would have cost five million dollars to repair, which is why it was abandoned, and the $24,000 a year that it costs to maintain Alcatraz now is mostly for surveillance, partly to barge in the 400,000 gallons of water that Bill Doherty and the Harts use every year (there is no water at all on Alcatraz, one impediment to development), and the rest to heat two apartments and keep some lights burning. The buildings seem quite literally abandoned. The key locks have been ripped from the cell doors and the big electrical locking mechanisms disconnected. The teargas vents in the cafeteria are empty and the paint is buckling everywhere, corroded by the sea air, peeling off in great scales of pale green and ocher. I stood for a while in Al Capone's cell, five by nine feet, number 200 on the second tier of B Block, not one of the view cells, which were awarded on seniority, and I walked through the solitary block, totally black when the doors were closed. "Snail Mitchel," read a pencil scrawl on the wall of Solitary 14. "The only man that ever got shot for walking too slow." Beside it was a calendar, the months penciled on the wall with the days scratched off, May, June, July, August of some unnumbered year.

Mr. Scott, whose interest in penology dates from the day his office acquired Alcatraz as a potential property, talked about escapes and security routines and pointed out the beach where Ma Barker's son Doc was killed trying to escape. (They told him to come back up, and he said he would rather be shot, and he was.) I saw the shower room with the soap still in the dishes. I picked up a yellowed program from an Easter service *(Why seek ye the living among the dead? He is not here, but is risen.)* and I struck a few notes on an upright piano with the ivory all rotted from the keys and I tried to imagine the prison as it had been, with the big lights playing over the windows all night long and the guards patrolling the gun galleries and the silverware clattering into a bag as it was checked in after meals, tried dutifully to summon up some distaste, some night terror of the doors locking and the boat pulling away. But the fact of it was that I liked it out there, a ruin devoid of human vanities, clean of human illusions, an empty place reclaimed by the weather where a woman plays an organ to stop the wind's whining and an old man plays ball with a dog named Duke. I could tell you that I came back because I had promises to keep, but maybe it was because nobody asked me to stay.

Didion, Joan. "Rock of Ages." *Patterns Plus*, Third Edition. Mary Lou Conlin, Editor. Houghton Mifflin Company, 1990, pp. 93–95. ISBN: 0-395-51691-9.

Suggestions for discussion and writing:

1. What is the dominant impression the author wishes to create?

2. Does Didion use comparison or contrast to heighten her descriptions?

3. How does the author use details in the first paragraph?

4. Discuss what Alcatraz must have been like during the 1930's and through to the 1950's.

5. Write an essay in which you describe Ellis Island when it was new.

ARGUMENT/PERSUASION

Definition:

Argument and persuasion are closely related but distinctly different. The use of argument is dependent upon *logic* and rational judgments over a long span, and is used to appeal to a reader's sense of *reason*. Persuasion, in contrast, is employed to arouse audience *emotion* over the short term. By definition, argumentation is the attempt to persuade readers to adopt a particular point of view, to make a decision, and to pursue a specific course of action. It is best to rely upon thoughtful argument when writing, yet, it is also necessary to understand the techniques of persuasive expression in order to be fully educated regarding the writing process.

Effective writers always include argument and persuasion in their works to some extent. As singular modes of development, both have some particular characteristics that a writer needs to understand if he wishes to be effective. When a writer wants to convince the reader that his thesis is correct or believable, he generally applies argument and/or persuasion to advance his statement. Despite the differences between argument and persuasion, it is important for a writer to understand that both, in application, are pretty much the same. The human individual is neither pure emotion nor pure mind, but rather one who responds to ideas in both an emotional and intellectual manner. As modes, argument and persuasion are perhaps the most important of all the writing techniques for the serious writer and ought to be used in almost every written expression.

Method:

There are four major steps in the use of argument:

establish the proposition;

analyze the proposition;

formulate the argument; and

prepare the brief.

The proposition, sometimes referred to as the thesis, is a clear, definite and concise statement of what is to be discussed. It is used to provide a point of contact for the writer's claim or assertion. A proposition ought to be stated in very specific and affirmative terms. The writer should make it sufficiently narrow so as to permit a definite point of contact. It is important to establish the proposition firmly and exactly.

The analysis of the proposition is based upon definite indications of the meanings and limitations of the proposition set forward for defense or attack. Define the terms used in the proposition clearly. This will insure that the reader has a clear understanding of the writer's words. This is called the universe of discourse from which the writer advances the major point of the argument. The writer should be sure to combine the definition of terms with a statement of the history of the question, and then offer supporting material which will serve as *logical evidence* for the proposition.

Next, the writer should arrange the major points of the proposition along with the supporting evidence in such a way that they will serve as a formulation of the argument. This is known as the formulation of proof, and at this point the writer depends heavily upon reasoning if the argument is to be effective. The formulation will work well with the usual rules of exposition and a combination of modes; however, it is most important to remember to rely upon an understanding of human nature when formulating the argument. The choice of order in the formulation will depend upon the writer's purpose and the nature of the intended audience.

Argument is almost entirely a matter of recognizing and revealing logical relationships between ideas. Preparing a brief in argument is useful, and serves to specify content and the order in which material will be discussed. The brief is similar to a sentence or paragraph type outline, but differs in that the writer utilizes conjunctions such as "for," most notably, in order to reveal specific developing relationships between ideas.

The four major steps in the use of argument are important. Each step is dependent upon straight forward, logical thinking. The success of argument in practical writing is closely related to the effective use of persuasion, but more importantly, it is wholly dependent upon *honest and thoughtful* analysis of the issue for debate. Remember that argument/persuasion as a mode is not to be used for quarreling nor advancing some devious purpose, but for convincing the reader of the correctness of an opinion or course of action that the writer deems desirable for the common good.

Major Points:

- Use logic, reason, and emotions
- Establish a proposition
- Analyze the proposition
- Formulate the argument
- Prepare the brief
- Offer logical evidence
- Be honest and thoughtful

LET'S BULLDOZE THE SUBURBS

Fred Powledge

Fred Powledge is a freelance writer who has worked on several newspapers as a reporter and editor. A native of North Carolina, he has published numerous articles and books on the topics of race relations, urban problems, social revolutions, and the environment. His works are often provocative, and that is precisely what makes his writings so fascinating.

For almost 30 years now, America has been systematically destroying the centers of her cities. In the name of urban renewal, we have declared choice parcels of downtown real estate to be slums and then forced their rightful owners—often stable but poor families and small businesses—to move away. We have sent bulldozers in at taxpayers' expense to flatten the old housing, and then we have given the cleared land away at bargain prices to the operators of parking garages, overpriced hospitals, and chain hotels, to the developers of high-rise bank buildings and luxury housing.

The downtowns thus "renewed" have become cold, juiceless mausoleums that the more well-to-do office workers pass through nervously when heading to and from their homes in the suburbs—suburbs that were built simultaneously with the urban-renewal program and at the expense of the cities and city-dwellers. For while our politicians were giving the downtowns away, they were also encouraging the construction of suburban rings (some call them nooses) around the cities to house the Americans who, to them, count: the white, young, middle- and upper-income citizens who fear and despise the black, the poor, the city.

Who despise *some* of the city. The suburbanites like to come downtown to collect their paychecks, to take advantage of the cultural offerings, to cruise for interracial sex, to go to the ballgames. So the politicians have built a series of interstate highways and peripheral expressways to serve the suburbanites. The incredible rationale was that the roads were essential for our civil defense.

The white, better-off Americans are still there in the suburbs, and the poor and black and despised are still there in the central cities. Discrimination and exclusion, far from abating, have only gotten worse. It is time, now, that the nation undertook a massive new effort to renew its citizens' lives and surroundings. It is time to systematically destroy suburbia.

The need for suburbia's annihilation should be obvious to any reasonable person who has the stomach to pass through its sacred precincts. Suburbia is, first of all, ugly—physically, socially, politically, intellectually, and emotionally ugly.

It is, and of right ought to be, an embarrassment to its residents. No one, to my knowledge, has ever bragged about living in suburbia.

Suburbia is where the police commit the grossest sins against the Constitution and where the seamiest political corruption may be found. It is the place where school board members routinely burn the "obscene" or "controversial" books by honored authors and then admit that they have never read them. Suburbia has a peculiar talent for bringing out the dumbest and worst in people.

Suburbia is as culturally alive as a turnip. It has no great museums or libraries of its own, and so its residents must go to the cities to keep their brains from ossifying. There are no great restaurants in suburbia. The only social institution that it *has* developed is the giant shopping center, our most fitting possible memorial to greed and bad taste. Suburbia's young people may be seen loitering day and night at these Eastgates and Westgates and asphalt-encrusted Green Acres, their glassy eyes reflecting the vacuity of the suburban landscape, their brains forever soft-boiled by the Muzak that issues from endless chains of K-Marts and Woolcos. Some young people manage to escape into the real world, but many do not. The only salvation for many of them is rock music and killer weed.

Suburbia is racist, and so most of those young people will never know contemporaries who are not socioeconomic duplicates of themselves. Suburbia was conceived largely as a place in which better-off whites might escape confrontations with blacks; so it is not surprising that even now Negroes make up a tiny portion of the suburban population. Similar exclusion prevails in religious and economic matters; such time-honored schemes as requirements that housing be built on minimum-sized plots of one or two acres make it certain that communities will be homogenized into lifelessness.

Suburbia is supremely wasteful at a time when civilization simply cannot afford to throw its resources away. Because there is no adequate public transportation and because suburban housing is largely single-family and one-story, it squanders and taints vast quantities of fragile land, air, water, and energy. It removes enormous areas of cropland from cultivation and replaces them with large numbers of people who have been trained to consume highly processed foods. Suburbia is parasitic, draining both the cities and the surrounding farmlands and forestlands of their resources and vitality and giving nothing in return.

And, as is the case with most shoddily built contraptions, suburbia is falling apart before its time. No one is surprised that the housing is disintegrating, but there's more: suburbia is discovering that there's no place to dump the sewage and garbage. The water's starting to taste funny, the kids have strange scars on their arms, crime is rampant, taxes are sky-high, transportation is an ordeal, and it takes half an hour to get out of Eastgate's parking lot. Education is becoming a joke, politics are corrupt, and the pollution is often worse than in the hated city. Surely it's time to do something swift and lasting to this slumland that festers out there beyond the city limits.

The obvious solution is a giant slum-clearance program similar to the one by which the central cities were stripped, flattened, and resold. Suburbia—its houses and highways and shopping centers—must be leveled to the ground from which it so recently oozed. But this time the profiteers must not be the bankers and builders and other special interests. This time the American public in general must benefit.

I propose a program by which almost all suburban land will be returned to its former state of wildness or agriculture. The people who live in suburbia will be paid equitable sums for their homes and carports, of course, and they will be free to move wherever they want, as long as it is outside of the officially designated Suburban Clearance Agency Region (SCAR). Some might want to establish totally new cities. Those who agree to return to the decaying central cities will receive the best deal: relocation incentives and technical assitance in rehabilitating abandoned urban housing.

This time the relocation will take place on a strictly non-discriminatory basis. It is certain that once the suburbanites move into the city, the concern and solicitude of the politicians and bankers will quickly follow them, as will adequate social services and other amenities. Thus *two* sets of slums simultaneously will be eradicated—the ones left behind in the suburbs and the ones that have existed all along in the cities.

Overnight the inner-city blocks will develop into solid, attractive housing stock. The cities will regain their financial stability. Mortgage money will finally become available inside the city limits. Employment rates will climb, since everyone who wants a job will be able to find one in either the construction or demolition industries. America will be on the move again.

In the territories that once were known as suburbia, the land will be encouraged to return to forest and pasture for the refreshment, recreation, and nutritional improvement of all Americans. It shouldn't take long to recrown these parks and woodlands with more fitting names: the New Rochelle Natural Area, for example, or Scarsdale National Forest. Maybe we'll discover a silver spring under the asphalt and aluminum siding of Silver Spring, Md., or sand in Sandy Springs, north of Atlanta. The names of all those suburban condotheques will finally start to reflect some reality—the Quail Hollows and Forest Hills and Hickory Groves. Maybe Deer Park will actually become a deer park, and perhaps that ominous split down Southern California's middle will miraculously heal once the weight of so much suburban excess is removed.

I don't think suburbia should be *completely* dismantled. Small tracts of housing should be offered free to poor, black, brown, red, yellow, and tan urban Americans as temporary vacation lodgings—as *pieds-à-terre,* literally, for people whose feet seldom have had opportunities to touch real earth. Some of the shopping centers can be retained for use as prisons or museums or educational institutions where the newly re-emerging environment might be studied. Some of the more garish shopping malls might serve especially well as grain silos or chicken coops or indoor feedlots.

And there should be a few suburban preserves—places where the suburban environment as we now know it can be retained for the enlightenment and amusement of posterity. These preserves will contain real, live suburban homes and suburban people, who go through their daily routines while their visitors—curious city residents out for the weekend, schoolchildren on field trips—look on. There they'll be: staggering home from the bar car, watching television with single- (not to mention simple-) minded devotion, wolfing down their Frozen Entrees and Tuna Helper and Kraft Miniature Marshmallows, riding around out front on their nasty little lawnmowers. These living museums will help future generations understand, better than any history book or television documentary could, why it was so necessary that the suburban slums be eradicated.

Powledge, Fred. "Let's Bulldoze the Suburbs." *Thinking in Writing*, Second Edition. Donald McQuade and Robert Atwan, Editors. Alfred A. Knopf, 1983, pp. 459–463. ISBN: 0-394-32819-1.

Suggestions for discussion and writing:

1. What is Powledge's purpose for writing the essay?
2. Does the author offer an indictment of suburbia?
3. How persuasive is Powledge's opening paragraph?
4. Does Powledge provoke the reader in an attempt to bring about change?
5. Write an essay about the suburbs, and attempt to persuade the reader to change his attitude or behavior regarding land use and the environment.

DEATH TO THE KILLERS

Mike Royko

Mike Royko writes a syndicated column for the Chicago
Daily News. *He has a large readership and strong feelings about social issues including the death penalty.*

Some recent columns on the death penalty have brought some interesting responses from readers all over the country.

There were, of course, expressions of horror and disgust that I would favor the quick dispatching of convicted murderers.

I really don't like to make fun of people who oppose the death penalty because they are so sincere. But I wish they would come up with some new arguments to replace the worn-out ones.

For example, many said something like this: "Wouldn't it be better to keep the killers alive so psychiatrists can study them in order to find out what makes them the way they are?"

It takes the average psychiatrist about five years to figure why a guy wants to stop for two drinks after work and won't quit smoking. So how long do you think it will take him to determine why somebody with an IQ of 92 decided to rape and murder the little old lady who lives next door?

Besides, we have an abundance of killers in our prisons— more than enough to keep all the nation's shrinks busy for the next 20 years. But shrinks aren't stupid. Why would they want to spend all that time listening to Willie the Wolfman describe his ax murders when they can get $75 an hour for listening to an executive's fantasies about the secretarial pool?

Another standard is: "The purpose of the law should be to protect society, not to inflict cruel retribution, such as the death penalty."

In that case, we should tear down all the prisons and let all the criminals go because most people would consider a long imprisonment to be cruel retribution—especially those who are locked up. Even 30 days in the Cook County Jail is no picnic.

And: "What gives society the right to take a life if an individual can't?" The individuals who make up society give it that right. Societies perform many functions that individuals can't. We can't carry guns and shoot people, but we delegate that right to police.

Finally: "The death penalty doesn't deter crime," I heard from a number of people who have a less detached view of the death penalty than many of the sensitive souls who oppose it.

For instance, Doris Porch wrote me about a man on Death Row in Tennessee. He hired men to murder his wife. One threw in a rape, free of charge.

Porch wrote: "My family had the misfortune of knowing this man (the husband) intimately. The victim was my niece. After her decomposed body was found in the trunk of her car, I made the trip to homicide with my sister."

Sharon Rosenfeldt of Canada wrote: "We know exactly what you are talking about because our son was brutally murdered and sexually abused by mass murderer Clifford Olson in Vancouver.

"Words can't explain the suffering the families of murder victims are left to live with. After two years, we're still trying to piece our lives back together mentally and spiritually."

Eleanor Lulenski of Cleveland said: "I'm the mother of one of the innocent victims. My son was a registered nurse on duty in an emergency room. A man walked in demanding a shot of penicillin. When he was told he would have to be evaluated by a physician, he stomped out, went to his car, came back with a shotgun and killed my son.

"He was sentenced to life, but after several years the sentence was reversed on a technicality—it being that at the time of his trial it was mentioned that this was his second murder."

And Susie James of Greenville, Miss.: "My tax dollars are putting bread into the mouth of at least one murderer from Mississippi who showed no mercy to his innocent victim.

"He caught a ride with her one cold February night. She was returning to her home from her job in a nursing home. She was a widow. The murderer, whom she had befriended, struck her on the head with a can of oil. Ignoring her pleas, he forced her through a barbed-wire fence into the woods at knifepoint. He stabbed her repeatedly, raped her and left her for dead.

"When the victim's son walked down the stairs to leave the courthouse after the guilty sentence had been uttered, he happened to look at the killer's mother.

She said: 'You buzzard, watching me.'

"'The murder victim was my mother.'"

There are many others. The mother of the boy who angered some drunken street thugs. They shot him and then ran him over repeatedly with a car. The mother whose son and daughter were beaten to death. The brother who remembers how his little sister would laugh as they played—until she was butchered.

They have many things in common. They suffered a terrible loss, and they live with terrible memories.

One other thing they share: The knowledge that the killers are alive and will probably remain alive and cared for by society.

Opponents of the death penalty should try explaining to these people just how cruel it is to kill someone.

Royko, Mike. "Death to the Killers." *Patterns Plus,* Third Edition, Mary Lou Conlin, Editor. Houghton Mifflin Company, 1990, pp. 369–371. ISBN: 0-395-51691-9

Suggestions for discussion and writing:

1. Discuss why Royko suggests that psychiatrists are not interested in investigating why people kill.

2. Does Royko use argument or persuasion to make his point?

3. Does the author refute the old argument that the death penalty will not deter murderers?

4. Write an essay in which you support or reject the death penalty.

5. Write an essay using persuasive techniques to arouse the reader's emotions.

THE SECONDARY MODES

Although not as important as the primary modes, utilization of the secondary modes is vital for the production of good written compositions. Like tools, the writer needs to know which modes to use at any given time in order to accomplish a specific task. These modes are used sometimes alone, and sometimes in combinations. The secondary modes, called the mixed modes, are employed by writers to blend the written piece so as to express the desired effect. The power behind the employment of the secondary modes is found in the hands of the individual writer, who like an artist, creates works that sometimes provoke, and other times satisfy and delight an audience. These modes are:

> **Example/Illustration**
>
> **Process Analysis**
>
> **Division and Classification**
>
> **Observation and Inference**
>
> **Comparison and Contrast**
>
> **Analogy**
>
> **Definition**
>
> **Cause and Effect**

EXAMPLE/ILLUSTRATION

Definition:

The writer uses example/illustration to make ideas more concrete and generalizations more specific. Example and illustration as modes are synonymous. A writer should use illustration to clarify or support a thesis. *Illustration,* often termed *example,* is used by a writer, not just to tell, but to *show what he wishes to express*. Clear illustration or example can often be employed to support the main points and convince the audience regarding the validity of the thesis. Either mode of development, when used properly, is one of the simplest and most effective ways for a writer to communicate ideas.

Method:

The main purpose for using example or illustration is to *make the general specific and the abstract concrete.* Example or illustration may be thought of as a part or pattern of something. Illustration can be used to *help explain something larger.* Included in a dictionary, for example, may be a definition for "mixed metaphor" as "a succession of metaphors that produce an incongruous and ludicrous effect." By itself that definition is somewhat vague. However, should the dictionary contain further exemplification such as "for example: his mounting ambition was soon bridled by a wave of opposition from a more stable group," then illustration has been employed to ensure that the precise meaning of the phrase "mixed metaphor" is understood. Illustration carries the thought from the abstract to the concrete.

The use of *illustration can add detail* to the writer's essay. Particular examples can be shown in sentences or paragraphs, and can be employed to make up an entire essay. The choice of examples is dependent upon the thesis. The examples ought to be carefully thought of as relevant additions for the clarification of the main idea the author wishes to advance. Importance should be given to the *positioning and timing* of the illustrations. Each point advanced should be illustrated clearly, and placement of examples usually works best at the beginning and end of the point of discussion.

Major Points:

- Show what the writer wishes to express
- Make the general specific and the abstract concrete
- Explain something larger
- Add detail
- Positioning and timing

THE FAMILY/CAREER PRIORITY PROBLEM

Ellen Goodman

A journalist and Pulitzer Prize winner, Ellen Goodman examines the question of how successful people handle career and family.

One day last week Ed Koch left his Greenwich Village apartment to take the M-6 bus downtown. About the same time he was being sworn in as mayor of New York City, my friend Carol was turning down a job as a top executive of a New York corporation.

On the surface, these two events seem to be totally unrelated, except for the fact that they took place in the same city. But I don't think they are. You see, Ed Koch is a bachelor, and my friend Carol is married and a parent, and there's a difference.

No, this isn't a story that ends with a one-line complaint from Carol: "If it hadn't been for you, I would have been a star." (Or a mayor, for that matter.) Nor is it a story of discrimination. Her husband didn't put his foot down. Her parents didn't form a circle around her shouting, "*Bad* mother, *bad!*" until she capitulated.

Carol chose. She wanted the promotion so much she could taste it. But the job came with weekends and evenings and traveling attached, and she didn't want to miss that time with her husband and sons. She couldn't do both. Knowing that didn't make it any easier.

Carol isn't the only one I know making these decisions. Another friend refused to move up a rung on the professional ladder because it would have meant uprooting his family and transferring his wife out of a career of her own. A third couple consciously put their careers on the back burner in order to spend time with the family they'd merged out of two previous marriages.

These were not bitter choices, but tough ones. As Carol said, it isn't possible to give overtime at work and decent time at home.

51

Once it was normal for a man to devote his energy entirely to his work, while his family was taken care of by his wife. Once men led the public lives and women the private lives. Now that gap is closing, and another one is growing between family people and single people.

Everywhere it seems that men and women who care the most about their private lives are living them that way, while the single people have become the new upwardly mobile.

In Washington you can see the difference. There, a twenty-eight-year-old bachelor such as White House aide David Rubinstein works more than sixteen hours a day and eats vending-machine meals, while a guy like Representative Lloyd Meeds (D-Washington) decides not to take his family through another congressional election fight, and drops out. There, despite the attempts of the Carters to encourage family time, the government still runs on excess. As one observer puts it, the only way to get the work done is to be single or to have a lousy marriage.

In New York the successful politicians (aside from Koch) now include Carol Bellamy, the single head of the city council, and Andrew Stein, the divorced borough president. The governor is a widower, the lieutenant governor is legally separated.

All around us the prototypical workaholics are single, with Ralph Nader leading the Eastern division, and Jerry Brown bringing up the West. And in the U.S. Senate last year there were enough divorces to justify legal insurance.

I don't think that this is something "movements" or legislation can solve. I am reminded of the moment in the movie *The Turning Point* when Anne Bancroft and Shirley MacLaine realize that they both wanted it all. These two women hadn't chosen in their lives between work and family in the classic sense, but between workaholism and family: between the sort of success that demands single-minded devotion to a goal and the sort of "balanced" life that includes family and work, but precludes overachieving. In the end the star was a bachelor.

The decisions they faced are the rock-bottom ones, the toughies. How do you divide the pie of your life—your own time and energy?

Today, the cast of characters is changing. It isn't only men in high-powered work lives and women at home. But the choices have remained the same. There seems to be an inherent contradiction between the commitment to become number one, the best, the first, and the commitment to a rich family life. A contradiction between family-first people and work-first people.

The irony is that we need decision-makers who care and understand about children and private lives. And I wonder how we will find them if the room at the top becomes a bachelor pad.

Goodman, Ellen. "The Family/Career Priority Problem." *Patterns Plus,* Third Edition. Mary Lou Conlin, Editor. Houghton Mifflin Company, 1990, pp. 133–135. ISBN: 0-395-51691-9.

Suggestions for discussion and writing:

1. What references does Goodman use to make her point in the essay?
2. How does Goodman use something small to explain something larger?
3. Discuss the modern trend of career mothers and single parent households.
4. Write an essay in which you give examples of the problems of balancing home and office.
5. Discuss the relationship of the title of Goodman's essay to the examples she uses.

ONE ENVIRONMENT, MANY WORLDS

Herbert and Judith Kohl

Herbert and Judith Kohl are school teachers. Herbert is the author of several books about education, and Judith is interested in animal behavior and archeology. The following is an excerpt from their book The View from the Oak.

Our dog Sandy is a golden retriever. He sits in front of our house all day waiting for someone to come by and throw him a stick. Chasing sticks or tennis balls and bringing them back is the major activity in his life. If you pick up a stick or ball to throw, he acts quite strangely. He looks at the way your body is facing and as soon as you throw something, he runs in the direction you seemed to throw it. He doesn't look at what you threw. His head is down and he charges, all ears. If your stick lands in a tree or on a roof, he acts puzzled and confused. He runs to the sound of the falling stick and sometimes gets so carried away that he will crash into a person or tree in the way as he dashes to the place he hears the stick fall. As he gets close, his nose takes over and smells the odor of your hand on the stick.

Once we performed an experiment to see how sensitive Sandy's nose really was. We were on a beach that was full of driftwood. There was one particular pile that must have had hundreds of sticks. We picked up one stick, walked away from the pile and then threw it back into the pile. It was impossible for us to tell with any certainty which stick we had originally chosen. So many of them looked alike to us that the best we could do was pick out seven sticks which resembled the one that had been thrown.

We tried the same thing with Sandy, only before throwing the stick we carved an X on it. Then we threw it, not once but a dozen times into the pile. Each time he brought back that stick. Once we pretended to throw the stick and he charged the driftwood pile without noticing that one of us still had the

54

stick. He circled the pile over and over, dug out sticks, became agitated but wouldn't bring another stick. It wasn't the shape or the size or look of the stick that he used to pick it out from all the others. It was the smell we left on the stick.

It is hard to imagine, but for dogs every living creature has its own distinctive smell. Each person can be identified by the smell left on things. Each of us gives off a particular combination of chemicals. We can detect the smell of sweat, but even when we are not sweating, we are giving off smells that senses finer than ours can detect.

The noses of people have about five million cells that sense smell. Dogs' noses have anywhere from 125 to 300 million cells. Moreover, these cells are closer to the surface than are cells in our noses, and more active. It has been estimated that dogs such as Sandy have noses that are a million times more sensitive than ours. Clothes we haven't worn for weeks, places we've only touched lightly indicate our presence to dogs. Whenever Sandy is left alone in the house, on our return we find him surrounded by our sweaters, coats, handkerchiefs, shirts. He surrounds himself with our smell as if to convince himself that we still exist and will return.

His ears are also remarkable. He can hear sounds that humans can't and at distances which are astonishing. It is hard for us to know and understand that world. Most of us don't realize that no two people's hands smell the same. Our ears are not the tuned direction finders his are. It takes a major leap of the imagination to understand and feel the world the way he does, to construct a complicated way of dealing with reality using such finely tuned smell and hearing. Yet his world is no more or less real than ours. His world and ours fit together in some ways and overlap in places. We have the advantage of being able to imagine what his experience is like, though he probably doesn't think too much about how we see the world. From observing and trying to experience things through his ears and nose we can learn about hidden worlds around us and understand behavior that otherwise might seem strange or silly.

The environment is the world that all living things share. It is what is—air, fire, wind, water, life, sometimes culture. The environment consists of all the things that act and are acted upon. Living creatures are born into the environment and are part of it too. Yet there is no creature who perceives all of what is and what happens. Sandy perceives things we can't, and we perceive and understand many things beyond his world. For a dog like Sandy a book isn't much different than a stick, whereas for us one stick is pretty much like every other stick. There is no one world experienced by all living creatures. Though we all live in the same environment, we make many worlds.

Kohl, Herbert and Judith. "One Environment, Many Worlds." *Models for Writers*, Second Edition, 1986. Alfred Rosa and Paul Eschholz, Editors. St. Martin's Press, pp. 186–188. ISBN: 0-312-53592-9.

Suggestions for discussion and writing:

1. What is the authors' purpose for writing this essay?

2. How do they use examples to give unity to the essay?

3. What would the environment be like without automobiles?

4. Discuss what is meant by "many worlds."

5. Write a brief essay in which you give examples of the many different college courses.

AT WAR WITH THE SYSTEM

Enid Nemy

A native of Canada, Enid Nemy spent many years working as a reporter and editor for various U.S. and Canadian newspapers. She is best known for her award-winning column, "New Yorkers, etc.," in The New York Times.

Business beware!

Do NOT trifle with Prof. David Klein.

Professor Klein looks like a nice, upper middle-class type. Most of the time he is. Sometimes he's not. Nice, that is.

"I behave reasonably outrageously by current standards," he admits without a hint of hedging or shilly-shallying.

Professor Klein has no middle-class hang-ups. He doesn't care about his credit rating (although it's still impeccable); he doesn't give a hoot whether business organizations and their employees think he's cheap or crazy, or both, and he isn't a bit abashed about making a scene, as long as the scene is quiet and well-bred.

Professor Klein is at war with the system "and if more people did what I do, business practices might improve," he said.

A distinguished looking man with a serious mien, twinkling eyes and a Vandyke beard, Mr. Klein began his campaign three or four years ago "when things began to deteriorate."

Take, for instance, one of his early experiences—a mere skirmish, but enough to whet the appetite.

The professor arrived at the Queen Elizabeth Hotel in Montreal after a tiring air trip and was told that his confirmed reservation could not be honored. There wasn't a room available. Sorry.

"I will give you three minutes to find me a room," he told the clerk quietly but firmly. "After three minutes, I am going to undress in the lobby, put on my pajamas and go to sleep on one of the sofas."

He got a room. He also got a lot of cheers and pats on the back from scores of other men waiting for overbooked rooms.

"But," Professor Klein recalled, a little sadly, "none of them would go ahead and do the same thing. I think I made my point in a reasonable, courteous way, but I also took a no-nonsense approach."

More recently, Mr. Klein, who has a master's degree from Columbia University, and is a professor of social science and human development at Michigan State University, has had several run-ins with retail operations. As a result, he has evolved his own charge system. He bills the store for any time he spends clearing up errors they have made on his orders or his account.

The current Klein rate is $10 a letter, a reasonable fee, he points out, when one considers not only his time but such expenses as photocopying checks that have already been cashed. Telephone calls are billed at $2 each. The fee scale is preinflation and is open to adjustment.

"I simply deduct the amount from my monthly charge account bill," he explained. "I add the total amount of time spent on letters and telephone calls when I'm billed incorrectly, or if orders come incomplete, or if merchandise is unsatisfactory.

"The complaint system has always struck me as terribly one-sided," he continued. "The store has people to handle complaints, and these people not only get paid to handle them but the basic cost of the department is added to the merchandise. The customer is not only paying a higher cost for everything because of store errors, but he or she is also expected to spend time writing or telephoning to clear up something that should never have happened in the first place."

The last time Professor Klein was put in the position of clearing up a complaint (one letter, three telephone calls) he deducted $15 from his bill at the end of the month. He knew what would happen, because he had had a similar reaction before.

A store representative telephoned, and the following conversation ensued:

Professor Klein: "Miss X, are you being paid by your employer to make this call?"

Miss X: "Well, yes."

Professor Klein: "Well, I'm not, so you will understand why I am not motivated to continue it. Goodbye."

Professor Klein figures that there are three courses of action the store might take, and as far as he is concerned, it doesn't matter which one they choose.

"If they want to sue me, fine," he said, cheerfully. "If they want to cancel my charge account, fine. And if they want to cancel my debt and give me back a zero balance, fine. They have a choice."

To date, the several stores that have encountered the Klein method of retaliation have, eventually, deducted his "fee" from the amount owed them.

"I do this as much as a matter of principle as a matter of making money," the professor said.

"A lot of middle-class people live in terror of being considered cheap," he said. "I don't worry about that. A lot of my solid middle-class friends say 'how do you dare do it . . . you'll ruin your credit rating.' They think that the least little cross-eyed look will ruin your credit rating. The fact is that a credit rating isn't as delicate as all that."

Professor Klein has several other antisystem, antiannoyance strategies. Among them are the following:

When buying an expensive item in a retail establishment that honors credit cards, he will hold up both his credit card and his checkbook and ask if the store will give him a three percent discount for cash. "They do," he said.

When unsolicited junk mail arrives, with a stamped reply card or envelope enclosed, he returns the card or envelope with his label stuck on it. The label reads: "This represents my effort to discourage unsolicited junk mail by increasing its cost to the sender." He had 1,000 labels printed for $1, but is somewhat discouraged because the volume of unsolicited mail continues unabated. "They can't read," he lamented.

He rarely pays cash for airline tickets because "if I put them on my credit card, it usually takes three or four months for the bill to arrive, and I can be earning interest on that money . . . no wonder Pan American is in trouble."

"One of the few nice things about being middle- or upper middle-class is that you have an enormous amount of clout," he said. "If people used it in the right way, they could make enormous changes in retailing, and in other practices."

Nemy, Enid. "At War With The System." *Models for Writers*, Second Edition, 1986. Alfred Rosa and Paul Eschholz, Editors. St. Martin's Press, pp. 190–193. ISBN: 0-312-53592-9.

Suggestions for discussion and writing:

1. Why does Nemy's narrator use words such as "retaliation" and "unsolicited"?
2. Does Nemy employ examples effectively?
3. Point out the main idea of the story and identify supporting examples.
4. Write an essay in which you discuss "antisystem, and antiannoyance strategies."
5. Write an essay using personal experience to show how you have fought back against a system.

PROCESS ANALYSIS

Definition:

Process analysis is used *to explain how* to do something, how something works, and how something happened. The mode of process analysis overlaps other writing techniques. More specifically, it closely resembles both narration and cause and effect. However, where narration as a mode is used to tell *what* happened, and cause and effect as a mode is employed to tell *why* something happened, process analysis actually is used by a writer as a form of *division* when he breaks a thing or concept into parts in order to explain *how* it functions as a process.

There are two basic types of process analysis:

(1) *directive*
and
(2) *explanatory,* sometimes referred to as speci-fied or informative.

Directive process analysis is used to explain how to do some-thing by offering directions such as how to bake a cake or how to ride a horse. *Explanatory process analysis is employed in order to offer information* such as how a cowhand saddles a horse or how oil is refined.

Method:

Whether directive or explanatory, process analysis is used to create a chronological order. Most processes can be divided into stages which in turn can be sub-divided into steps. This part of process analysis is similar to classification and divi-sion. The process for making a cake may take three stages such as mixing, baking, and icing. There are steps within the stages of the baking where it is necessary to preheat the oven, grease the baking pan, and let the cake bake for forty-five minutes. Following a tight chronological order, the writer should be sure to cover the stages in sequence, and each step of the stage in detail.

The writer should specify each step of the process and give reasons why each step is important. This ensures that the reader can comprehend fully what is being explained. It is important for the reader to understand how the process is put together if he is to grasp how it works. Process analysis can be applied to any number of operations, functions, or actions, and for each different application it will be necessary for the writer to develop a distinctive sequence of stages and steps. The writer's decision whether to use directive or explanatory process analysis is dependent upon the subject at hand. Process analysis is one of the most methodical and instructive ways to develop an essay. It is also one of the few modes where use of the first-person narrative is proper, although it is still better to write in the third-person for all essays of a formal nature.

Major Points:

- Explain how something is done or works
- Directive process analysis; tell how through directions
- Explanatory process analysis; give information
- Stages and steps

THE HIBERNATION OF THE WOODCHUCK

Alan Devoe

Alan Devoe (1909–1955) was a naturalist best known for his book on animal behavior, Lives Around Us *(1942). The following essay is an excellent example of process analysis, as the author takes the reader through the gradual process of hibernation.*

The woodchuck's hibernation usually starts about the middle of September. For weeks he has been foraging with increased appetite among the clover blossoms and has grown heavy and slow-moving. Now, with the coming of mid-September, apples and corn and yarrow tops have become less plentiful, and the nights are cool. The woodchuck moves with slower gait, and emerges less and less frequently for feeding trips. Layers of fat have accumulated around his chest and shoulders, and there is thick fat in the axils of his legs. He has extended his summer burrow to a length of nearly thirty feet, and has fashioned a deep nest-chamber at the end of it, far below the level of the frost. He has carried in, usually, a little hay. He is ready for the Long Sleep.

When the temperature of the September days falls below 50 degrees or so, the woodchuck becomes too drowsy to come forth from his burrow in the chilly dusk to forage. He remains in the deep nest-chamber, lethargic, hardly moving. Gradually, with the passing of hours or days, his coarse-furred body curls into a semicircle, like a foetus, nose-tip touching tail. The small legs are tucked in, the hand-like clawed forefeet folded. The woodchuck has become a compact ball. Presently the temperature of his body begins to fall.

In normal life the woodchuck's temperature, though fluctuant, averages about 97 degrees. Now, as he lies tight-curled in a ball with the winter sleep stealing over him, this body heat drops ten degrees, twenty degrees, thirty. Finally, by the time the snow is on the ground and the woodchuck's winter dormancy has become complete, his temperature is

63

only 38 or 40. With the falling of the body heat there is a slowing of his heartbeat and his respiration. In normal life he breathes thirty or forty times each minute; when he is excited, as many as a hundred times. Now he breathes slow and slower—ten times a minute, five times a minute, once a minute, and at last only ten or twelve times in an hour. His heartbeat is a twentieth of normal. He has entered fully into the oblivion of hibernation.

The Long Sleep lasts, on an average, about six months. For half a year the woodchuck remains unmoving, hardly breathing. His pituitary gland is inactive; his blood is so sluggishly circulated that there is an unequal distribution in the chilled body; his sensory awareness has wholly ceased. It is almost true to say that he has altered from a warm-blooded to a cold-blooded animal.

Then, in the middle of March, he wakes. The waking is not a slow and gradual thing, as was the drifting into sleep, but takes place quickly, often in an hour. The body temperature ascends to normal, or rather higher for a while; glandular functions instantly resume: the respiration quickens and steadies at a normal rate. The woodchuck has become himself again, save only that he is a little thinner, and is ready at once to fare forth into the pale spring sunlight and look for grass and berries.

Such is the performance each fall and winter, with varying detail, of bats and worms and bears, and a hundred other kinds of creature. It is a marvel less spectacular than the migration flight of hummingbirds or the flash of shooting stars, but it is not much less remarkable.

Devoe, Alan. "The Hibernation of the Woodchuck." *Thinking in Writing*, Second Edition. Donald McQuade and Robert Atwan, Editors. Alfred A. Knopf, 1983, pp. 366–367. ISBN: 0-394-32819-1.

Suggestions for discussion and writing:

1. What is Devoe's purpose?
2. Is this informational process analysis?
3. What major steps does Devoe explain?
4. Discuss the reasons for the woodchuck's changing behavior.
5. Write an essay in which you explain the dream process.

HOW TO SURVIVE A HOTEL FIRE

R. H. Kauffman

R.H. Kauffman was born in Portland, Oregon in 1941. While a captain in the Los Angeles Fire Department, he produced a booklet entitled Caution: Hotels Could be Hazardous to Your Health, *which now exceeds 44 million copies in print. The following excerpt from his booklet is an example of clear process analysis.*

As a firefighter, I have seen many people die in hotel fires. Most could have saved themselves had they been prepared. There are *over 10,000 hotel fires per year* in the United States. In 1979, the latest year for which figures are available, there were 11,500 such fires, resulting in 140 deaths and 1,225 injuries.

Contrary to what you have seen in the movies, fire is not likely to chase you down and burn you to death. It's the by-products of fire—smoke and panic—that are almost always the causes of death.

For example, a man wakes up at 2:30 A.M. to the smell of smoke. He pulls on his pants and runs into the hallway—to be greeted by heavy smoke. He has no idea where the exit is, so he runs first to the right. No exit. Where is it? Panic sets in. He's coughing and gagging now; his eyes hurt. He can't see his way back to his room. His chest hurts; he needs oxygen desperately. He runs in the other direction, completely disoriented. At 2:50 A.M. we find him . . . dead of smoke inhalation.

Remember, the presence of smoke doesn't necessarily mean that the hotel will burn down. Air-conditioning and air-exchange systems will sometimes pick up smoke from one room and carry it to other rooms or floors.

Smoke, because it is warmer than air, will start accumulating at the ceiling and work its way down. The fresh air you should breathe is near the floor. What's more, smoke is extremely irritating to the eyes. Your eyes will take only so much irritation, then they will close and you won't be able to open them.

Your other enemy, panic—a contagious, overpowering terror—can make you do things that could kill you. The man in the foregoing example would not have died if he had known what to do. Had he found out beforehand where the exit was—four doors down on the left—he could have gotten down on his hands and knees close to the floor, where the air is fresher.

Then, even if he couldn't keep his eyes open, he could have felt the wall as he crawled, counting doors.

Here are my rules for surviving hotel fires:

Know where the exits are. As soon as you drop your luggage in your room, turn around and go back into the hallway to check for an exit. If two share a room, both should locate the exit. Open the exit door. Are there stairs or another door beyond? As you return to your room, count the doors you pass. Is there anything in the hallway that would be in your way—an ice machine, maybe? This procedure takes very little time and, to be effective, it must become a habit.

Become familiar with your room. See if your bathroom has an exhaust fan. In an emergency you can turn it on to help remove smoke. Check the window. If it opens, look outside. Do you see any ledges? How high up are you?

Leave the hotel at the first sign of smoke. If something awakens you during the night, investigate it before you go back to sleep. In a hotel fire near Los Angeles airport, one of the guests was awakened by people yelling but went back to bed thinking it was a party. He nearly died in bed.

Always take your key. Don't lock yourself out of your room. You may find conditions elsewhere unbearable. Get in the habit of putting the key in the same place. The night stand, close to the bed, is an excellent spot.

Stay on your hands and knees. If you do wake up to smoke, grab your key from the night stand, roll off the bed and crawl toward the door. Even if you could tolerate the smoke when standing, don't. Save your eyes and lungs for as long as possible. Five feet up, the air may already be full of carbon monoxide. If the door isn't hot, open it slowly and check the hallway.

Should you decide to leave, close the door behind you. Most doors take hours to burn. They are excellent fire shields, so close every one you go through.

Make your way to the exit. Stay against the wall closest to the exit, counting doors as you pass.

Don't use the elevator. Elevator shafts extend through all floors of a building, and easily fill with smoke and carbon monoxide. Smoke, heat, and fire do odd things to elevator controls. Several years ago a group of firemen used an elevator in responding to a fire on a 20th floor. They pushed No. 18, but the elevator shot past the 18th floor and opened on the 20th—to an inferno that killed the firemen.

If you can't go down, go up. When you reach the exit stairwell and begin to descend, hang on to the handrail as you go. People may be running and they could knock you down.

Sometimes smoke gets into the stairwell. If it's a tall building, the smoke may not rise very high before it cools and becomes heavy, or "stacked." You could enter the stairwell on the 23rd floor and find it clear, then as you descend, encounter smoke. Do not try to run through it; people die that way. Turn around and walk up.

When you reach the roof, prop open the door. (This is the *only* time to leave a door open.) Any smoke in the stairwell can now vent itself. Find the windward side of the building (the side that the wind is blowing *from)* and wait until the firefighters reach you. Don't panic if you can't get out onto the roof because the door is locked. Many people have survived by staying put in the stairwell until the firefighters arrived. Again, don't try to run through the smoke.

Look before you leap. If you're on the ground floor, of course, just open the window and climb out. From the next floor you might make it with only a sprained ankle, but you must jump out far enough to clear the building. Many people hit windowsills and ledges on the way down, and cartwheel to the ground. If you're any higher than the third floor, chances are you won't survive the fall. You would probably be better off staying inside, and fighting the fire.

If you can't leave your room, fight the fire. If your door is too hot to open or the hallway is completely filled with smoke, don't panic. First, open the window to help vent any smoke in your room. (Don't break the window; if there is smoke outside, you may need to close it.)

If your phone is still working, call the fire department. (Do not assume it has been notified. Incredibly enough, some hotels will not call the fire department until they verify whether there is really a fire and try to put it out themselves.)

Flip on the bathroom fan. Fill the tub with water. Wet some sheets or towels, and stuff them into the cracks around your door to keep out smoke. Fill your ice bucket or wastebasket with water from the bathtub and douse the door and walls to keep them cool. If possible, put your mattress up against the door and secure it with the dresser. Keep everything wet. A wet towel tied around your nose and mouth can be an effective filter of smoke particles. Swing a wet towel around the room; it will help clear the smoke. If there is fire outside the window, remove the drapes, move away as much combustible material as you can, and throw water around the window. Use your common sense, and keep fighting until help arrives.

Kauffman, R.H. "How to Survive a Hotel Fire." *Models for Writers*, Second Edition. Alfred Rosa and Paul Eschholz, Editors. St. Martin's Press, 1986, pp. 256–259. ISBN: 0-312-53592-9.

Suggestions for discussion and writing:

1. What is Kauffman's purpose?
2. At what point in the essay does Kauffman begin to give directions regarding steps to be taken?
3. Is this essay written in the first-, second-, or third-person?
4. Discuss the process for taking an in-class writing examination.
5. Write a short process analysis article of the operations of driving a car.

DIVISION AND CLASSIFICATION

Definition:

Division and classification, although often used together, are two distinct processes. The use of *division* as a mode starts with the writer taking *a single subject and breaking it into components or parts.* The parts are different, sometimes interdependent, and essential as elements for understanding the function of the whole.

Classification begins when the writer is discussing *many subjects* and *grouping them according to their similarities.* Division and classification are affected directly by the writer's purpose. Whatever the writer wishes to prove or explain determines the class of things or ideas to be divided and classified.

Remember that *to divide is to separate* a class of things into categories, while *to classify is to group* separate things into those categories.

Method:

The writer should *clearly identify the purpose of the essay* and then select the appropriate principle of division in accordance with that purpose. For example, to determine the composition of the local government through division, the writer ought to consider logically:

political party—	Democrat
	Republican
	Independent
educational background—	college
	high school
	elementary
annual income—	$100,000 per year
	$ 50,000 per year
	$ 25,000 per year

This is the reasonable way to divide, rather than separating people according to their breakfast food cereals or the colors of their clothes.

69

Next, the writer should *divide the subject into mutually exclusive categories.* A component should belong to one category only, as it would be confusing to classify politicians, for example, as men, women, and joggers. The writer should *make the division and classification complete,* and account for all components in a given subject class. It is important to *make a concise clear statement of conclusion based upon the division and classification.* For example, if the writer has divided bicycles into three categories of racing, mountain, and pleasure bikes respectively, then a logical inference may be drawn that these three are more important for advancing the author's purpose than are children's tricycles or circus style unicycles. The author's concise statement ought to be something like "There are three important types of bicycles." Even further, the author may have classified racing bikes as more important than mountain bikes, and mountain bikes as more important than pleasure bikes. One can see that the bicycles have been first divided according to types, and second, grouped in terms of importance and types.

Classification is used to *sort out information about a subject, and put it into logically related categories.* Classification is most often employed when a subject is complex or extensive. A librarian, for example, classifies books into categories such as education, science, fiction, and the like. Even shopping in the supermarket requires knowledge of classification as the various foods are grouped and designated by signs. Consider the confusion that would prevail if neither the librarian nor the grocer were to classify books or food.

Major Points:

- Identify purpose
- Select appropriate principle of division
- Divide the subject into mutually exclusive categories
- Break a single subject into parts
- Divide many subjects according to similarities
- Make the division and classification complete
- Make a clear statement of conclusion based upon the division and classification

FOUR KINDS OF READING

Donald Hall

Donald Hall is a first-rate freelance writer, poet, play-wright, editor, and teacher. His article is an example of classification and the mutual dependence he places upon reading and writing.

Everywhere one meets the idea that reading is an activity desirable in itself. It is understandable that publishers and librarians—and even writers—should promote this assumption, but it is strange that the idea should have general currency. People surround the idea of reading with piety, and do not take into account the purpose of reading or the value of what is being read. Teachers and parents praise the child who reads, and praise themselves, whether the text be *The Reader's Digest* or *Moby Dick*. The advent of TV has increased the false values ascribed to reading, since TV provides a vulgar alternative. But this piety is silly; and most reading is no more cultural nor intellectual nor imaginative than shooting pool or watching *What's My Line*.

It is worth asking how the act of reading became something to value in itself, as opposed for instance to the act of conversation or the act of taking a walk. Mass literacy is a recent phenomenon, and I suggest that the aura which decorates reading is a relic of the importance of reading to our great-great-grandparents. Literacy used to be a mark of social distinction, separating a small portion of humanity from the rest. The farm laborer who was ambitious for his children did not daydream that they would become schoolteachers or doctors; he daydreamed that they would learn to read, and that a world would therefore open up to them in which they did not have to labor in the fields fourteen hours a day for six days a week in order to buy salt and cotton. On the next rank of society, ample time for reading meant that the reader was free from the necessity to spend most of his waking hours making a living of any kind. This sort of attitude shades into the contemporary man's boast of his wife's cultural activities.

When he says that his wife is interested in books and music and pictures, he is not only enclosing the arts in a delicate female world; he is saying that he is rich enough to provide her with the leisure to do nothing. Reading is an inactivity, and therefore a badge of social class. Of course, these reasons for the piety attached to reading are never acknowledged. They show themselves in the shape of our attitudes toward books; reading gives off an air of gentility.

It seems to me possible to name four kinds of reading, each with a characteristic manner and purpose. The first is reading for information—reading to learn about a trade, or politics, or how to accomplish something. We read a newspaper this way, or most textbooks, or directions on how to assemble a bicycle. With most of this sort of material, the reader can learn to scan the page quickly, coming up with what he needs and ignoring what is irrelevant to him, like the rhythm of the sentence, or the play of metaphor. Courses in speed reading can help us read for this purpose, training the eye to jump quickly across the page. If we read *The New York Times* with the attention we should give a novel or a poem, we will have time for nothing else, and our mind will be cluttered with clichés and dead metaphor. Quick eye-reading is a necessity to anyone who wants to keep up with what's happening, or learn much of what has happened in the past. The amount of reflection, which interrupts and slows down the reading, depends on the material.

But it is not the same activity as reading literature. There ought to be another word. If we read a work of literature properly, we read slowly, and we hear all the words. If our lips do not actually move, it's only laziness. The muscles in our throats move, and come together when we see the word "squeeze." We hear the sounds so accurately that if a syllable is missing in a line of poetry we hear the lack, though we may not know what we are lacking. In prose we accept the rhythms, and hear the adjacent sounds. We also register a track of feeling through the metaphors and associations of words. Careless writing prevents this sort of attention, and becomes offensive. But the great writers reward this attention. Only by the full exercise of our powers to receive language can we absorb their intelligence and their imagination. This kind of reading goes through the ear—though the eye takes in the print, and decodes it into sound—to the throat and the understanding, and it can never be quick. It is slow and sensual, a deep pleasure that begins with touch and ends with the sort of comprehension that we associate with dream.

Too many intellectuals read in order to reduce images to abstractions. With a philosopher one reads slowly, as if it were literature, but much time must be spent with the eyes turned away from the pages, reflecting on the text. To read literature this way is to turn it into something it is not—to concepts clothed in character, or philosophy sugar-coated. I think that most literary intellectuals read this way, including the brighter Professors of English, with the result that they miss literature completely, and concern themselves with a minor discipline called the history of ideas. I remember a course in Chaucer at my University in which the final exam largely required the identification of a hundred or more fragments of Chaucer, none as long as a line. If you liked poetry, and read Chaucer through a couple of times slowly, you found yourself knowing them all. If you were a literary intellectual, well-informed about the great chain of being, chances are you had a difficult time. To read literature is to be intimately involved with the words on the page, and never to think of them as the embodiments of ideas which can be expressed in other terms. On the other hand, intellectual writing—closer to mathematics on a continuum that has at its opposite pole lyric poetry—requires intellectual reading, which is slow because it is reflective and because the reader must pause to evaluate concepts.

But most of the reading which is praised for itself is neither literary nor intellectual. It is narcotic. Novels, stories and biographies—historical sagas, monthly regurgitations of book clubs, four- and five-thousand word daydreams of the magazines—these are the opium of the suburbs. The drug is not harmful except to the addict himself, and is no more injurious to him than Johnny Carson or a bridge club, but it is nothing to be proud of. This reading is the automated daydream, the mild trip of the housewife and the tired businessman, interested not in experience and feeling but in turning off the possibilities of experience and feeling. Great literature, if we read it well, opens us up to the world, and makes us more sensitive to it, as if we acquired eyes that could see through things and ears that could hear smaller sounds. But by narcotic reading, one can reduce great literature to the level of *The Valley of the Dolls*. One can read *Anna Karenina* passively and inattentively and float down the river of lethargy as if one were reading a confession magazine: "I Spurned My Husband for a Count."

I think that everyone reads for narcosis occasionally, and perhaps most consistently in late adolescence, when great readers are born. I remember reading to shut the world out, away at a school where I did not want to be; I invented a word to name my disease: "bibliolepsy," on the analogy of narcolepsy. But after a while the books became a window on the world, and not a screen against it. This change doesn't always happen. I think that late adolescent narcotic reading accounts for some of the badness of English departments. As a college student, the boy loves reading and majors in English because he would be reading anyway. Deciding on a career, he takes up English teaching for the same reason. Then in graduate school he is trained to be a scholar, which is painful and irrelevant, and finds he must write papers and publish them to be a Professor—and at about this time he no longer requires reading for narcosis, and he is left with nothing but a Ph.D. and the prospect of fifty years of teaching literature; and he does not even like literature.

Narcotic reading survives the impact of television, because this type of reading has even less reality than melodrama; that is, the reader is in control: once the characters reach into the reader's feelings, he is able to stop reading, or glance away, or superimpose his own daydreams. The trouble with television is that it writes its own script. Literature is often valued precisely because of its distance from the tangible. Some readers prefer looking into the text of a play to seeing it performed. Reading a play, it is possible to stage it oneself by an imaginative act; but it is also possible to remove it from real people. Here is Virginia Woolf, who was lavish in her praise of the act of reading, talking about reading a play rather than seeing it: "Certainly there is a good deal to be said for reading *Twelfth Night* in the book if the book can be read in a garden, with no sound but the thud of an apple falling to the earth, or of the wind ruffling the branches of the trees." She sets her own stage; the play is called *Virginia Woolf Reads Twelfth Night in a Garden.* Piety moves into narcissism, and the high metaphors of Shakespeare's lines dwindle into the flowers of an English garden; actors in ruffles wither, while the wind ruffles branches.

Hall, Donald. "Four Kinds of Reading." *Thinking in Writing,* Second Edition, 1983. Donald McQuade and Robert Atwan, Editors. Alfred A. Knopf, pp. 162–166. ISBN: 0-394-32819-1.

Suggestions for discussion and writing:

1. Are Hall's four categories clear?
2. Does Hall make a distinction between reading literature and speed reading?
3. Does Hall develop each category in an effective way?
4. Discuss the mutual dependence between reading and writing.
5. Write an essay in which you explore the different values in reading.

THREE DISCIPLINES
FOR CHILDREN

John Holt

John Holt is a contemporary writer who, although having few literary credits to his background, uses classification and division most expertly. His article is quite informative as he employs categories to depict how life works in part.

A child, in growing up, may meet and learn from three different kinds of disciplines. The first and the most important is what we might call the Discipline of Nature or of Reality. When he is trying to do something real, if he does the wrong thing or doesn't do the right one, he doesn't get the result he wants. If he doesn't pile one block right on top of another, or tries to build on a slanting surface, his tower falls down. If he hits the wrong key, he hears the wrong note. If he doesn't hit the nail squarely on the head, it bends, and he has to pull it out and start with another. If he doesn't measure properly what he is trying to build, it won't open, close, fit, stand up, fly, float, whistle, or do whatever he wants it to do. If he closes his eyes when he swings, he doesn't hit the ball. A child meets this kind of discipline every time he tries to *do* something, which is why it is so important in school to give children more chances to do things, instead of just reading or listening to someone talk (or pretending to). This discipline is a great teacher. The learner never has to wait long for his answer; it usually comes quickly, often instantly. Also it is clear, and very often points toward the needed correction; from what happened he cannot only see what he did was wrong, but also why, and what he needs to do instead. Finally, and most important, the giver of the answer, call it Nature, is impersonal, impartial, and indifferent. She does not give opinions, or make judgments; she cannot be wheedled, bullied, or fooled; she does not get angry or disappointed; she does not praise or blame; she does not remember past failures or hold grudges; with her one always gets a fresh start, this time is the one that counts.

The next discipline we might call the Discipline of Culture, of Society, of What People Really Do. Man is a social, a cultural animal. Children sense around them this culture, this network of agreements, customs, habits, and rules binding the adults together. They want to understand it and be a part of it. They watch very carefully what people around them are doing and want to do the same. They want to do right, unless they become convinced they can't do right. Thus children rarely misbehave seriously in church, but sit as quietly as they can. The example of all those grownups is contagious. Some mysterious ritual is going on, and children, who like rituals, want to be part of it. In the same way, the little children that I see at concerts or operas, though they may fidget a little, or perhaps take a nap now and then, rarely make any disturbance. With all those grownups sitting there, neither moving nor talking, it is the most natural thing in the world to imitate them. Children who live among adults who are habitually courteous to each other, and to them, will soon learn to be courteous. Children who live surrounded by people who speak a certain way will speak that way, however much we may try to tell them that speaking that way is bad or wrong.

The third discipline is the one most people mean when they speak of discipline—the Discipline of Superior Force, of sergeant to private, of "you do what I tell you or I'll make you wish you had." There is bound to be some of this in a child's life. Living as we do surrounded by things that can hurt children, or that children can hurt, we cannot avoid it. We can't afford to let a small child find out from experience the danger of playing in a busy street, or of fooling with the pots on the top of a stove, or of eating up the pills in the medicine cabinet. So, along with other precautions, we say to him, "Don't play in the street, or touch things on the stove, or go into the medicine cabinet, or I'll punish you." Between him and the danger too great for him to imagine we put a lesser danger, but one he can imagine and maybe therefore want to avoid. He can have no idea of what it would be like to be hit by a car, but he can imagine being shouted at, or spanked, or sent to his room. He avoids these substitutes for the greater danger until he can understand it and avoid it for its own sake. But we ought to use this discipline only when it is necessary to protect the life, health, safety, or well-being of people or other living creatures, or to prevent destruction of things that people care about. We ought not to assume too long, as we usually do, that a child cannot understand the real nature of the danger from which we want to protect him. The sooner he avoids the danger, not to escape our punishment, but as a matter of good sense, the better. He can learn that faster than we think. In Mexico, for example, where people drive their cars with a good deal of spirit, I saw many children no older than five or four walking unattended on the streets. They understood about cars, they knew what to do. A child whose life is full of the threat and fear of punishment is locked into babyhood. There is no way for him to grow up, to learn to take responsibility for his life and acts. Most important of all, we should not assume that having to yield to the threat of our superior force is good for the child's character. It is never good for anyone's character. To bow to superior force makes us feel impotent and cowardly for not having had the strength or courage to resist. Worse, it makes us resentful and vengeful. We can hardly wait to make someone pay for our humiliation, yield to us as we were once made to yield. No, if we cannot always avoid using the Discipline of Superior Force, we should at least use it as seldom as we can.

Holt, John. "Three Disciplines for Children." *Patterns Plus*, Third Edition. Mary Lou Conlin, Editor. Houghton Mifflin Company, 1990, pp. 175–177. ISBN: 0-395-51691-9.

Suggestions for discussion and writing:

1. How is the main idea of Holt's essay expressed?
2. Does Holt use some sense of order in his essay?
3. Are there different classes of nature?
4. Discuss the importance of categorization.
5. Write an essay in which you divide and classify automobiles.

OBSERVATION AND INFERENCE

Definition:

Observation and inference as a mode of writing ought to be thought of as two distinct units. These two units of observation and inference are elementary aspects of the human process of thought and inquiry. The writer, when considering the subject at hand, has a responsibility to provide the audience with factual evidence to support each assertion made. Most writers, regardless of purpose, rely upon three essential sources of knowledge:

direct observation, the information collected from first-hand experience;

recollection, the remembrance of what was once observed;

testimony, the reports of what others have observed or recalled.

Human thought usually follows a pattern of observation and inference. It generally begins with what is perceived by an observer's senses during an experience, and ends with what is suggested by that experience. Based upon observations of experiences, humans draw inferences about a given subject. Observation is relatively simple, while conversely, drawing an inference can be highly speculative. Seeing a sofa, for example, is not really an observation of great revelation. Noting a dog hair on the sofa, however, is quite a different story. It is possible to make a logical statement of inference based upon that particular observation. Even though the observer cannot see the dog upon the sofa, the sight of the dog hair is sufficient information for the observer to add to previous knowledge about dogs, comfort, and sofas, which then permits an inferred conclusion that the dog most probably was resting upon the couch.

The writer uses observation to help the audience move from one level of what is known, to what is not yet known. Inference is used to aid the writer and audience by filling the gaps and allowing the writer to make a statement about what is absent based upon what is present.

79

Method:

The writer utilizes observation to provide facts. There are four basic kinds of facts to employ when writing expository essays:

private facts which are those facts that can be experienced by an individual such as a backache or the taste of spinach;

public facts which are facts that people of the world have agreed to such as the meaning of a year or a day;

scientific facts such as the principles of physics or mathematics which are subject to change at any time;

primary facts such as how many teeth in the mouth of a human or how many fingers on one hand.

The writer has the responsibility to provide convincing, factual evidence to support each assertion made. By using the factual categories in tandem with direct observation, recollection, and testimony, it is possible to present logical conclusions based upon observation and inference.

Major Points:

- Use direct observation, recollection, and testimony
- Provide private, public, scientific, and primary facts to support each assertion

ANATOMY OF A MARTIAN

Isaac Asimov

Isaac Asimov is known as one of the world's most prolific writers. Born in Russia and raised in Brooklyn, N.Y., he wrote over 300 books. Known primarily as a science-fiction writer, his essays and short stories are paradigms for readers. Trained as a biochemist, Asimov applied sound scientific principles along with logical inferences to present fiction that borders on the edge of reality. He wrote to inform his audience through accuracy and clarity.

Conditions are so different on Mars and—to our earth-centered feelings—so inferior from those on earth that scientists are confident no intelligent life exists there. If life on Mars exists at all (the probability of which is small, but not zero) it probably resembles only the simplest and most primitive terrestrial plant life.

Still, even granted that the likelihood of complex life is virtually nonexistent, we can still play games and let our fancy roam. Let us suppose that we are told flatly: "There is intelligent life on Mars, roughly man-shaped in form." What reasonable picture can we draw on the basis of what we now know of Mars—bearing always in mind that the conclusions we reach are not to be taken seriously, but only as an exercise in fantasy?

In the first place, Mars is a small world with a gravitational force only two-fifths of the earth. If the Martian is a boned creature, those bones can be considerably slenderer than ours and still support a similar mass of material (an inevitable mechanical consequence of decreased weight). Therefore, even if the torso itself were of human bulk, the legs and arms of the Martian would seem grotesquely thin to us.

Objects fall more slowly in a weak gravitational field and thus the Martians could afford to have slower reflexes. Therefore, they would seem rather slow and sleepy to us (and they might be longer-lived because of their less intense fight with gravitation). Since things are less top-heavy in a low-gravity world, the Martian would probably be taller than earth people. The Martian backbone need not be so rigid as ours and might have two or three elbow-like joints, making stooping from his (possible) eight-foot height more convenient.

The Martian surface has been revealed by the Mars-probe, Mariner IV, to be heavily pockmarked with craters, but the irregularities they introduce are probably not marked to a creature on the surface. Between and within the craters, much of the surface is probably sandy desert. Yellow clouds obscuring the surface are occasionally detected and, in the 1920s, the astronomer E. M. Antoniadi interpreted these as dust storms. To travel over shifting-sands, the Martian foot (like that of the earthly camel) would have to be flat and broad. That type of foot, plus the weak gravity, would keep him from sinking into the sand.

As a guess, the feet might be essentially triangular, with three toes set at 120° separation, with webbing between. (No earthly species has any such arrangement, but it is not an impossible one. Extinct flying reptiles, such as the pterodactyl, possessed wings formed out of webbing extending from a *single* line of bones.) The hands would have the same tripod development, each consisting of three long fingers, equally spaced. If the slender finger bones were numerous, the Martian finger would be the equivalent of a short tentacle. Each might end in a blunt swelling (like that of the earthly lizard called the gecko), where a rich network of nerve endings, as in human fingertips, would make it an excellent organ for touching.

The Martian day and night are about as long as our own, but Mars is half again as far from the sun as we are, and it lacks oceans and a thick atmosphere to serve as heat reservoirs. The Martian surface temperature therefore varies from an occasional 90° Fahrenheit, at the equatorial noon, down to a couple of hundred degrees below zero, by the end of the frigid night. The Martian would require an insulating coating. Such insulation might be possible with a double skin; the outer one, tough, horny, and water impervious, like that of an earthly reptile; the inner one, soft, pliable, and richly set with blood vessels, like that of an earthly man. Between the two skins would be an air space which the Martian could inflate or deflate.

At night the air space would be full and the Martian would appear balloonlike. The trapped air would serve as an insulator, protecting the warmth of the body proper. In the warm daytime, the Martian would deflate, making it easier for his body to lose heat. During deflation, the outer skin would come together in neat, vertical accordion pleats.

The Martian atmosphere, according to Mariner IV data, is extremely thin, perhaps a hundredth the density of our own and consisting almost entirely of carbon dioxide. Thus, the Martian will not breathe and will not have a nose, though he will have a strongly muscled slit—in his neck, perhaps—through which he can pump up or deflate the air space.

What oxygen he requires for building his tissue structure must be obtained from the food he eats. It will take energy to obtain that oxygen, and the energy supply for this and other purposes may come directly from the sun. We can picture each Martian equipped with a capelike extension of tissue attached, perhaps to the backbone. Ordinarily, this would be folded close to the body and so would be inconspicuous.

During the day, however, the Martian may spend some hours in sunlight (clouds are infrequent in the thin, dry Martian air) with his cape fully expanded, and resembling a pair of thin, membranous wings reaching several feet to either side. Its rich supply of blood vessels will be exposed to the ultraviolet rays of the sun, and these will be absorbed through the thin, translucent skin. The energy so gained can then be used during the night to enable the necessary chemical reactions to proceed in his body.

Although the sun is at a great distance from Mars, the Martian atmosphere is too thin to absorb much of its ultraviolet, so that the Martian will receive more of these rays than we do. His eyes will be adapted to this, and his chief pair, centered in his face, will be small and slitlike to prevent too much radiation from entering. We can guess at two eyes in front, as in the human being, since two are necessary for stereoscopic vision—a very handy thing to have for estimating distance.

It is very likely that the Martian will also be adapted to underground existence, for conditions are much more equable underground. One might expect therefore that the Martian would also have two large eyes set on either side of his head, for seeing by feeble illumination. Their function would be chiefly to detect light, not to estimate distance, so they can be set at opposite sides of the head, like those of an earthly dolphin (also an intelligent creature), and stereoscopic vision in feeble light can be sacrificed. These eyes might even be sensitive to the infrared so that Martians can see each other by the heat they radiate. These dim-vision eyes would be enormous enough to make the Martian face wider than it is long. In daytime, of course, they would be tightly closed behind tough-skinned lids and would appear as rounded bulges.

The thin atmosphere carries sound poorly, and if the Martian is to take advantage of the sense of hearing, he will have to have large, flaring, trumpetlike ears, rather like those of a jackrabbit, but capable of independent motion, flaring open and furling shut (during sandstorms, for instance).

Exposed portions of the body, such as the arms, legs, ears, and even portions of the face which are not protected by the outer skin and the airtrap within, could be feathered for warmth in the night.

The food of the Martian would consist chiefly of simple plant life, which would be tough and hardy and which might incorporate silicon compounds in its structure so that it would be gritty indeed. The earthly horse has teeth with elaborate grinding surfaces to handle coarse, gritty grass, but the Martian would have to carry this to a further extreme. The Martian mouth, therefore, might contain siliceous plates behind a rounded opening which could expand and contract like a diaphragm of a camera. Those plates would work almost like a ball mill, grinding up the tough plants.

Water is the great need. The entire water supply on Mars is equal only to that contained in Lake Erie, according to an estimate cited by astronomer Robert S. Richardson. Consequently, the Martian would hoard the water he consumes, never eliminating it as perspiration or wastes, for instance. Wastes would appear in absolutely dry form and would be delivered perhaps in the consistency, even something of the chemical makeup, of earthly bricks.

The Martian blood would not be used to carry oxygen, and would contain no oxygen-absorbing compound, a type of substance which in earthly creatures is almost invariably strongly colored. Martian blood, therefore, would be colorless. Thus the Martian skin, adapted to ultraviolet and absorbing it as an energy source, would not have to contain pigment to ward it off. The Martian therefore would be creamy in color.

The extensible light-absorbing cape, particularly designed for ultraviolet absorption, might reflect longwave visible light as useless. This reflected light could be yellowish in color. This would cause our Martian to seem to be (when he was busily absorbing energy from solar radiation) a dazzling white creature with golden wings and occasional feathers.

So ends our speculation—in a vision of Martian forms not so far removed from the earthman's fantasies of the look of angels.

Asimov, Isaac. "Anatomy of a Martian." *Thinking in Writing*, Second Edition. Donald McQuade and Robert Atwan, Editors. Alfred A. Knopf, 1983, pp. 63–67. ISBN: 0-394-32819-1.

Suggestions for discussion and writing:

1. What does Asimov use as a basis for his inferences?
2. Are Asimov's inferences based upon scientific facts?
3. Can Asimov see Mars?
4. Describe a creature that could live on Venus.
5. Observe some natural event and then write an essay withholding your conclusions to the end.

CLEVER HANS

Emily Hahn

*Emily Hahn was born in St. Louis, Missouri, in 1905.
Educated at the University of Wisconsin, Columbia University, and Oxford University, she is well prepared to
write in a formal and clear style. The following article grew
out of her studies in animal behavior and communication.*

Language is only one form of communication. We ourselves
have perfected several codes of facial expressions and ges-
tures; anyone who doubts it has only to watch speakers on the
television screen when the sound is off. Other species have
developed various methods of communicating with one another. Some of these methods depend on sight, some on
sound, some on scent, and some on touch. For a long time, we
could not imagine such different modes; if an animal did not
produce at least a fair approximation of our method of signal-
ling—namely, speech—we gave up trying to get in touch with
it. We could see and hear communication going on in the
songs of birds, in the silent communication of horses, in the
play of dogs and cats, but we stood outside. Over the years,
many people have entertained a wistful regret that all this life
was hidden from us—a circumstance that helps to explain the
eagerness with which the world has always received rumors
that some animal has been vouchsafed the gift of speech.

A generation before Descartes published his strictures on
reason in animals, the Western world was fascinated by a
white horse named Morocco, owned by one Mr. Banks, of
London. Morocco, though not able to talk, evidently understood speech, for he did practically everything Banks told him
to; among the men who marvelled at his talents were
Shakespeare, Ben Jonson, and Sir Walter Raleigh. He could
dance in time to music. If somebody rolled the dice and Banks
asked Morocco what the total was, the horse tapped the
ground with a hoof the right number of times. He could
answer yes-or-no questions the same way, tapping once for

yes and twice for no. He answered correctly when he was asked how old a bystander might be: the person would whisper his age to Banks, and, sure enough, Morocco would tap out the right answer. Very seldom did he make a mistake. Finally, a contemporary writer who specialized in magic and juggling tricks and knew how the thing was done wrote about it. He observed that Morocco, while he was performing, never took his eyes off his master, Banks, and that Banks stood very still until the horse had pawed the ground the right number of times, and then, unobtrusively, he shrugged one shoulder. Whenever this happened, Morocco stopped tapping his hoof.

Milbourne Christopher, a modern writer whose subject is magic and the like, has traced the career of Morocco and recounted two incidents that he admits may or may not be true. It was said that Banks took his wonderful animal to France and started giving performances there, but was soon arrested and charged with practicing witchcraft. This happened in Orléans. He was condemned to death by the court, but Morocco saved him by going up to a high official and kneeling down to him. Later, in Rome, according to an equally doubtful story that Christopher tells, Banks and Morocco were both burned at the stake.

Banks's horse may have been the first of his kind, but there has been a long line of similarly conditioned performing animals, not necessarily equines. Near the end of the eighteenth century, New Yorkers were able to watch a star billed as the Learned Dog, and an equally accomplished pig was rapturously received here a few years later. Under the auspices of one Mr. William Frederick Pinchbeck, the pig could play card games, selecting any one of a number of cards that lay on the floor. In time, Pinchbeck himself exposed the secret method he used to aid the animal in making its selections: whenever the pig's snout hovered over the right card, the man sniffed, making a noise that was just loud enough for the animal to hear but was lost on the audience. Horses, however, seem to have been the most popular, for there were many of them. Christopher lists the Learned Little Horse, who entertained the public in Glasgow in 1764; the Military Horse of Knowledge, who could be seen in 1780 in England; Spottie, who appeared in Baltimore in 1807; and an Arabian animal,

Mahomet, whose trainer, a Mr. E. L. Probasco, had taught him to add and subtract as fast as any human being, and who was first exhibited in 1889.

It was now time for the appearance of the most famous learned horse of all, Clever (or, in his native German, Kluge) Hans. The difference between Hans and his renowned predecessors was that nobody seems to have thought of him as one of the show animals; he was in a class by himself. Or perhaps it was the people astonished by Hans's feats who were in a special class, insulated from the mob: they were intellectuals, who might never have heard of Spottie or Mahomet, and it is quite possible that they hadn't. At any rate, it seems certain that Hans's owner, a former mathematics teacher named Wilhelm von Osten, trained his animal in good faith. And the professors who examined Hans and wrote long papers about him did not link him up with the marvellous horses of Mr. Banks and Mr. Probasco, though much of what Hans did was just like the feats of those other animals.

Every day, the wonderful horse was exhibited in a paved courtyard that adjoined his stall, in a northern district of Berlin, next to Mr. von Osten's house. About noon, there would gather in the courtyard a select company of people who had been invited by Mr. von Osten—mathematicians, musicians, psychology professors, and others who had a valid reason for being there. No charge was ever made for the show; it was not, as I have said, that kind of thing at all. The pair of them would enter from the stall—Wilhelm von Osten, a white-haired man who was somewhere between sixty-five and seventy, holding Hans's bridle, and Hans himself, a good-looking trotting horse in fine condition, wearing merely a girth strap, a snaffle, and light headgear. He seemed very docile, though it was rumored that he sometimes showed flashes of bad temper. Von Osten handled him gently, with soft, encouraging words; he never used a whip. Now and then, after a correct reply, he would slip Hans a piece of bread or a carrot. If von Osten's questions were of the yes-or-no type, they were answered by a nod or a headshake on the part of Hans, who also indicated "up" and "down" with his head. Other questions, which were answered with hoof-tapping, had to be posed within the limits of the vocabulary with which he was familiar, but its scope was fairly wide and increased day by day. By means of the code that von Osten had taught him, the horse would transpose into numbers a variety of concepts—letters of the alphabet, tones of the musical scale, the names of playing cards—and use them appropriately. He mastered the cardinal numbers from one to one hundred and the ordinals to ten. He solved arithmetic problems. He could read German, though Mr. von Osten taught him only lower-case letters: when placards with several written words were put in front of him and he was told to do so, he indicated one word or another by pointing to it with his nose. He knew the value of all German coins. He carried the entire yearly calendar in his head and could give you the right date for any day you might mention. He recognized people from their photographs. In music, he had absolute tone consciousness, and could recognize a note sung to him as C, D, etc. (within the once-accented scale of C-major). There seemed no limit to his powers.

Not surprisingly, Hans captured the public fancy in Germany. He was the subject of popular songs, and people could buy picture postcards of him and bring home little toy Hanses for the children. Nevertheless, there were some who doubted. Though no one had ever seen any signals pass between Mr. von Osten and his horse, there simply had to be signals, the skeptics said. Somebody suggested that the old mathematics master might be emitting the new X-rays that everybody was talking about. Or was it that mysterious thing called "hypnotic suggestion"? At length, it was agreed that a thorough scientific inquiry should be made into the matter. Mr. von Osten, after a time, promised to cooperate with the examiners, and a number of men, some familiar with Hans and some who were not so intimate with the horse and his master participated in the experiments. Two of the latter were Professor Stumpf, a psychologist, who was director of the Psychological Institute of the University of Berlin, and Oskar Pfungst, one of Stumpf's co-workers at the Psychological Institute, who later wrote a book about Hans. The rules were drawn up: every now and then, one of the gentlemen was to ask Hans something to which he himself did not have the answer. Also, the interrogators were to be switched from time to time. The stage was set, and the men arranged themselves with a questioner standing to Hans's right, equipped with bread, carrots, and lumps of sugar. With all due solemnity, a card with the figure 8 on it was produced and shown to the horse in such a way that the questioner couldn't see it. Hans tapped out fourteen. Next time, the questioner was allowed to look at the card. It was 8 again—and Hans tapped out eight. The next card said 4, and the questioner didn't see it. Hans tapped eight again. Whenever the questioner didn't see the card, Hans was wrong almost every time. Whenever he did, the horse was almost always right. There was no blinking at these facts: Hans could not count. Reading tests got the same results: Whenever the questioner didn't see the words, Hans didn't know them, but he made no mistakes when the man did see the words. So Hans couldn't read, either. He failed the test on calculation of dates; he failed in music, which was tested by someone playing a harmonica that spanned the once-accented octave.

Poor von Osten became increasingly dismayed as he saw his wonderful horse fail time after time. Perhaps, he suggested, the secret lay in sound waves emitted by the questioner. No, it was later decided, that could not be the explanation, because at times it wasn't necessary to speak aloud to Hans; he would start tapping before the question was uttered. Just to make sure, however, they tried him with earmuffs. The earmuffs made no difference. No, it couldn't be sound waves. However mysteriously he did it, the gentlemen agreed, Hans did get hold of visual signals. To try the idea out, they put blinkers on him. Something different happened immediately. Hans didn't care for the blinkers, and made what were described as strenuous efforts to regain a view of his questioner, raging and tearing at the lines when they tried to tie him and make him stand still. Furthermore, his record of answers now became woefully bad. When they took the blinkers off, Hans calmed down. They asked him questions in the old way, and now, at last, they noticed something that had never been observed before—that when a problem was posed to the horse he had a peculiar way of watching his questioner very closely, instead of looking at the object under consideration: the card or whatever it was.

Now that the examiners knew where to look, they soon had their solution: Hans was watching his questioner's involuntary movements. Having set a problem, the questioner unconsciously leaned forward to count the hoof taps, and when the proper number had been reached, he relaxed; that is, he straightened himself with a slight upward jerk of the head. It was the smallest possible movement, but it was enough for Hans.

The discovery had wide repercussions in the scientific world. Even today, researchers in the field of animal awareness are apt to say to one another over the results of some experiment, "You're sure that wasn't just a Clever Hans syndrome?" The affair may well have discouraged many people who wanted to find out more about animal communication.

Hahn, Emily. "Clever Hans." *Thinking in Writing*, Second Edition. Donald McQuade and Robert Atwan, Editors. Alfred A. Knopf, 1983, pp. 68–73. ISBN: 0-394-32819-1.

Suggestions for discussion and writing:

1. Which inferences drawn from observation are false?
2. What reasoning process is used to draw an inference?
3. What can you infer from Hahn's background?
4. Discuss how people communicate without using words.
5. Write an essay in which you make observations and inferences regarding a classmate.

COMPARISON AND CONTRAST

Definition:

Comparison and contrast is a mode used to demonstrate both the *similarities* and *differences* between two or more subjects. It is important to understand that comparison is used to show similarities while contrast is employed to depict differences. When used as a singular mode, the writer *explains* and *clarifies* subjects in relation to each other.

Method:

Comparison and contrast as a writing technique is used to achieve one of two purposes:

(1) the writer may wish to explain the similarities and differences between subjects or ideas in order *to clarify;*

(2) or he may want to *explain and evaluate* subjects or ideas so as to set forth their respective *advantages and disadvantages.*

When employing the explanatory mode, the writer should be objective and not take a position regarding the relative merits of the subject or idea. When using the evaluative method, the writer ought to make his position clear, and offer some conclusion regarding the subject or idea.

Generally, the writer should *classify the subjects* to be compared and contrasted by *arranging them in groups.* This ensures that the subjects are comparable. It would be a waste of time to compare a horse and a flea, as the two are obviously different. It is quite another matter, however, when the two are grouped into a class such as creatures with more than two legs. Then, it is quite simple to show their respective similarities and differences.

There are two basic ways to arrange subjects. One is *block-by-block,* sometimes called *subject-by-subject,* and the other is *point-by-point.*

The block-by-block approach is useful when a writer wishes to simplify the comparison and contrast. Comparing and contrasting a horse and a pony can be achieved easily by explaining all the characteristics of block 1, the horse, and block 2, the pony.

Example: block 1: Horse:
                       point 1: size
                       point 2: strength
                       point 3: productivity

             block 2: Pony:
                       point 1: size
                       point 2: strength
                       point 3: productivity

The writer may remain objective and end the comparison and contrast at this point or he may wish to evaluate and render a conclusion regarding the advantages and disadvantages involved.

The point-by-point method is used by a writer to explain each item, one at a time, in respect to the relative merits of the thing or things compared. When using this approach the writer should alternate back and forth explaining each point carefully.

Example: point 1: size: horse
                                         pony

             point 2: strength: horse
                                         pony

             point 3: productivity: horse
                                         pony

Again, the writer may remain objective by leaving the comparison and contrast at this juncture in the writing or he may wish to offer a conclusion regarding preference, benefit, and advantages and disadvantages at this point. This method is most advantageous for in-depth evaluation.

The writer has a third option of mixing comparison and contrast, which is most often the case when using comparison and contrast as a mode. For example, the writer can, by using comparison and contrast, discuss in block form various aspects of both horses and ponies. Block 1 might be used to compare the common traits of both animals, as well as their ranking in a class of equine creatures. Block 2 might be discussed in terms of the contrasts between the two animals in the sense of temperament and manageability.

Example: block 1:   compare: common traits
                                              ranking

                  block 2:   contrast: temperament
                                              manageability

As with the block-by-block, and point-by-point techniques, the mixed method can also end objectively or with some sort of a conclusion on the part of the writer regarding the advantages and disadvantages of the subject or idea.

Major Points:
- Show similarities and differences
- Explain and clarify
- Explain and evaluate
- Classify subjects
- Make block-by-block or point-by-point analysis
- Show advantages and disadvantages

GRANT AND LEE:
A STUDY IN CONTRASTS

Bruce Catton

Bruce Catton (1899–1978) was a journalist who worked for several newspapers, including the Cleveland Plain Dealer. *He won the Pulitzer Prize and the National Book Award in 1954 for his work* A Stillness at Appomattox. *An expert on the Civil War, he had over a dozen books published regarding the topic.*

When Ulysses S. Grant and Robert E. Lee met in the parlor of a modest house at Appomattox Court House, Virginia, on April 9, 1865, to work out the terms for the surrender of Lee's Army of Northern Virginia, a great chapter in American life came to a close, and a great new chapter began.

These men were bringing the Civil War to its virtual finish. To be sure, other armies had yet to surrender, and for a few days the fugitive Confederate government would struggle desperately and vainly, trying to find some way to go on living now that its chief support was gone. But in effect it was all over when Grant and Lee signed the papers. And the little room where they wrote out the terms was the scene of one of the poignant, dramatic contrasts in American history.

They were two strong men, these oddly different generals, and they represented the strengths of two conflicting currents that, through them, had come into final collision.

Back of Robert E. Lee was the notion that the old aristocratic concept might somehow survive and be dominant in American life.

Lee was tidewater Virginia, and in his background were family, culture, and tradition . . . the age of chivalry transplanted to a New World which was making its own legends and its own myths. He embodied a way of life that had come down through the age of knighthood and the English country squire. America was a land that was beginning all over again, dedicated to nothing much more complicated than the rather hazy belief that all men had equal rights, and should have an equal chance in the world. In such a land Lee stood for the feeling that it was somehow of advantage to human society to have a pronounced inequality in the social structure. There should be a leisure class, backed by ownership of land; in turn, society itself should be keyed to the land as the chief source of wealth and influence. It would bring forth (according to this ideal) a class of men with a strong sense of obligation to the community; men who lived not to gain advantage for themselves, but to meet the solemn obligations which had been laid on them by the very fact that they were privileged. From them the country would get its leadership; to them it could look for the higher values—of thought, of conduct, of personal deportment—to give it strength and virtue.

Lee embodied the noblest elements of this aristocratic ideal. Through him, the landed nobility justified itself. For four years, the Southern states had fought a desperate war to uphold the ideals for which Lee stood. In the end, it almost seemed as if the Confederacy fought for Lee; as if he himself was the Confederacy . . . the best thing that the way of life for which the Confederacy stood could ever have to offer. He had passed into legend before Appomattox. Thousands of tired, underfed, poorly clothed Confederate soldiers, long-since past the simple enthusiasm of the early days of the struggle, somehow considered Lee the symbol of everything for which they had been willing to die. But they could not quite put this feeling into words. If the Lost Cause, sanctified by so much heroism and so many deaths, had a living justification, its justification was General Lee.

Grant, the son of a tanner on the Western frontier, was everything Lee was not. He had come up the hard way, and embodied nothing in particular except the eternal toughness and sinewy fiber of the men who grew up beyond the mountains. He was one of a body of men who owed reverence and obeisance to no one, who were self-reliant to a fault, who cared hardly anything for the past but who had a sharp eye for the future.

These frontier men were the precise opposites of the tide-water aristocrats. Back of them, in the great surge that had taken people over the Alleghenies and into the opening Western country, there was a deep, implicit dissatisfaction with a past that had settled into grooves. They stood for democracy, not from any reasoned conclusion about the proper ordering of human society, but simply because they had grown up in the middle of democracy and knew how it worked. Their society might have privileges, but they would be privileges each man had won for himself. Forms and patterns meant nothing. No man was born to anything, except perhaps to a chance to show how far he could rise. Life was competition.

Yet along with this feeling had come a deep sense of belonging to a national community. The Westerner who developed a farm, opened a shop or set up in business as a trader, could hope to prosper only as his own community prospered—and his community ran from the Atlantic to the Pacific and from Canada down to Mexico. If the land was settled, with towns and highways and accessible markets, he could better himself. He saw his fate in terms of the nation's own destiny. As its horizons expanded, so did his. He had, in other words, an acute dollars-and-cents stake in the continued growth and development of his country.

And that, perhaps, is where the contrast between Grant and Lee becomes most striking. The Virginia aristocrat, inevitably, saw himself in relation to his own region. He lived in a static society which could endure almost anything except change. Instinctively, his first loyalty would go to the locality in which that society existed. He would fight to the limit of endurance to defend it, because in defending it he was defending everything that gave his own life its deepest meaning.

The Westerner, on the other hand, would fight with an equal tenacity for the broader concept of society. He fought so because everything he lived by was tied to growth, expansion, and a constantly widening horizon. What he lived by would survive or fall with the nation itself. He could not possibly stand by unmoved in the face of an attempt to destroy the Union. He would combat it with everything he had, because he could only see it as an effort to cut the ground out from under his feet.

So Grant and Lee were in complete contrast, representing two diametrically opposed elements in American life. Grant was the modern man emerging; beyond him, ready to come on the stage, was the great age of steel and machinery, of crowded cities and a restless, burgeoning vitality. Lee might have ridden down from the old age of chivalry, lance in hand, silken banner fluttering over his head. Each man was the perfect champion of his cause, drawing both his strengths and his weaknesses from the people he led.

Yet it was not all contrast, after all. Different as they were—in background, in personality, in underlying aspiration—these two great soldiers had much in common. Under everything else, they were marvelous fighters. Furthermore, their fighting qualities were really very much alike.

Each man had, to begin with, the great virtue of utter tenacity and fidelity. Grant fought his way down the Mississippi Valley in spite of acute personal discouragement and profound military handicaps. Lee hung on in the trenches at Petersburg after hope itself had died. In each man there was an indomitable quality . . . the born fighter's refusal to give up as long as he can still remain on his feet and lift his two fists.

Daring and resourcefulness they had, too; the ability to think faster and move faster than the enemy. These were the qualities which gave Lee the dazzling campaigns of Second Manassas and Chancellorsville and won Vicksburg for Grant.

Lastly, and perhaps greatest of all, there was the ability, at the end, to turn quickly from war to peace once the fighting was over. Out of the way these two men behaved at Appomattox came the possibility of a peace of reconciliation. It was a possibility not wholly realized, in the years to come, but which did, in the end, help the two sections to become one nation again . . . after a war whose bitterness might have seemed to make such a reunion wholly impossible. No part of either man's life became him more than the part he played in their brief meeting in the McLean house at Appomattox. Their behavior there put all succeeding generations of Americans in debt. Two great Americans, Grant and Lee— very different, yet under everything very much alike. Their encounter at Appomattox was one of the great moments of American history.

Catton, Bruce. "Grant and Lee: A Study in Contrasts." *The Resourceful Writer*, Second Edition, 1990. Suzanne S. Webb, Editor. Harcourt Brace Jovanovich, Publishers, pp. 213–216. ISBN: 0-15-576633-3.

Suggestions for discussion and writing:

1. Why does Catton contrast the two men before comparing them?
2. What might happen if comparison preceded contrast?
3. Does Catton inform, express, or persuade by using this method?
4. Discuss the value of comparative shopping.
5. Compare and contrast two of your favorite instructors.

STALLONE vs. SPRINGSTEEN

Jack Newfield

Jack Newfield is a freelance writer interested in the contemporary American scene. The following article first appeared in Playboy Magazine *in 1986 under the subtitle of "Which Dream Do You Buy?"*

Bruce Springsteen and Sylvester Stallone are the two great working-class heroes of American mass culture. Springsteen had the best-selling album of 1985 and Stallone has the second most successful movie. On the surface, they share stunning similarities of biceps, bandannas, American flags, Vietnam themes, praise from President Reagan and uplifting feelings of national pride. Bumper stickers proclaim, BRUCE—THE RAMBO OF ROCK.

But beneath the surface—and between the lines—these two American heroes of the eighties are sending opposite messages. They are subtly pulling the 18-to-35-year-old generation toward two competing visions of the American future.

Stallone's *Rocky* and *Rambo* films—especially the latter—are about violence and revenge in a context of fantasy. Rambo never pays a price in body bags or pain or blood or doubt or remorse or fear. The enemy is stereotyped and therefore dehumanized. The emotions Stallone liberates are hostility and aggression: Audiences come out of the theater wanting to kick some Commie ass in Nicaragua.

By contrast, the essential human feeling Springsteen liberates is empathy—compassion for the common man trapped in the dead-end world of the hourly wage. The realistic words of Springsteen's best songs are about the hurt of unemployed workers; about reconciliation with estranged parents through understanding *their* lives; about staying hopeful even though experience falls short of the American dream.

In *Rambo* Stallone depicts the Vietnam veteran as a killing machine, a deranged, rampaging executioner. In "Born in the U.S.A.," Springsteen depicts the Vietnam veteran as neglected—wanting to be reintegrated into society as a normal person but getting the brush-off from a bureaucrat at the Veterans Administration. Recall the misunderstood and mis-heard words of the Springsteen anthem:

> Got in a little hometown jam,
> So they put a rifle in my hand.
> Sent me off to a foreign land
> To go and kill the yellow man. . . .
> Come back home to the refinery.
>
> Hiring man says, "Son, if it was up to me. . . .
> "Went down to see my VA man;
> He said, "Son, don't you understand now?"
> I had a brother at Khé Sanh
> Fighting off the Viet Cong.
> They're still there; he's all gone.
> He had a woman he loved in Saigon—
> I got a picture of him in her arms now. . . .

The difference between Stallone and Springsteen is per-haps best illuminated by reading an essay George Orwell wrote in 1945, before either Stallone or Springsteen was born. In the essay, "Notes on Nationalism," Orwell makes a distinc-tion between nationalism and patriotism and then suggests that they are, in fact, opposites.

> By "nationalism" I mean first of all the habit of assum-ing that human beings can be classified like insects and that whole blocks of millions or tens of millions of people can confidently be labeled "good" or "bad." But secondly—and this is much more important—I mean the habit of identify-ing oneself with a single nation or other unit, placing it beyond good and evil and recognizing no other duty than that of advancing its interests. Nationalism is not to be confused with patriotism . . . since two different and even opposing ideas are involved. By "patriotism" I mean a devotion to a particular place and a particular way of life, which one believes to be the best in the world but has no wish to force upon other people. Patriotism is of its nature defensive, both militarily and culturally. Nationalism, on the other hand, is inseparable from the desire for power. . . .
>
> It can plausibly be argued, for instance—it is even probably true—that patriotism is an inoculation against nationalism.

Stallone as Rambo snarls, "Damn Russian bastards" and kills a few more. Springsteen introduces "This Land Is Your Land," the first encore at all his concerts, as "the greatest song ever written about America," and then reminds his fans, "Remember, *nobody wins unless everybody wins.*" That's one difference between nationalism and patriotism.

Stallone manipulates American's feelings of frustration over the lost Vietnam war and helps create a jingoistic climate of emotion in which a future war might be welcomed. Springsteen asks us to honor the neglected and rejected Vietnam veterans, so that we won't glide gleefully into the next war without remembering the real cost of the last one. That's a second difference between nationalism and patriotism.

"It's a right-wing fantasy," said Stallone, talking to *Time* about last summer's big hit. "What Rambo is saying is that if they could fight again, it would be different." He added that he was looking for another "open wound" as a site for a sequel, possibly Iran or Afghanistan.

Ron Kovic is a paraplegic author and Vietnam veteran. As an honored guest at Springsteen's opening-night concert last August at the Giants' stadium in New Jersey, Kovic told reporters, "I've been sitting in this wheelchair for the past 18 years. And I can only thank Bruce Springsteen for all he has done for Vietnam veterans. 'Born in the U.S.A.' is a beautiful song that helped me personally to heal." The difference between looking for another open wound as a movie backdrop and creating music that is healing—that's a third distinction between nationalism and patriotism. . . .

Nationalism, as defined by Orwell, is an intoxicating but essentially negative emotion, because it is, by its very nature, intolerant. It does not respect the rights of minorities or the dignity of neighbors. It is a will to power that negates complexity. Its most extreme avatars are monstrous lunatics such as Khomeini, Qaddafi, Botha, Farrankhan and Kahane.

The milder form of nationalism, as represented by Stallone, is less harmful. Stallone doesn't have Governmental power, and he doesn't push the issue; he usually retreats behind his movie character and tells most interviewers he is nonpolitical.

But the messages his images communicate to masses of impressionable young people sometimes do have damaging consequences. For example, the week *Rambo,* with its negative stereotypes of Asians, opened in Boston last spring, there were two incidents in which Southeast Asian refugees were badly beaten up by gangs of white youths.

In the more recent *Rocky IV*—which Stallone wrote, directed and starred in—the villainous foe is a Russian who fights dirty, takes illegal steroid injections and wears a black mouthpiece. Cleverly named Ivan Drago, he is depicted as a robotlike extension of the Evil Empire. Critics have written that it is the most simplistic and one-dimensional of all the *Rocky* movies. It lacks the interesting subplots and realistic blue-collar atmosphere of the original *Rocky,* with its loan shark and neighborhood gym; this time, Stallone literally and figuratively wraps himself in the American flag—proving that sequels are the last refuge of nationalists.

The worst features of Stallone's nationalism are the values it enshrines and reinforces: racism, violence, militarism and—possibly most subversive of all—simplicity. The convergence of these emotions can make war and foreign intervention seem like a sporting event. Or a movie.

Bruce Springsteen's patriotism is rooted in a different set of values, apparent in his songs: the old-fashioned virtues of work, family, community, loyalty, dignity, perseverance, love of country. His fundamental theme is the gap between America's promise and performance and his resilient faith in the eventual redemption of that promise. He sees America as it is, with all its jobless veterans, homeless people and urban ghettos. And he retains his idealism *in spite of everything,* because his patriotism has room for paradox. At a Springsteen concert, one song makes you want to cheer for America, the next makes you want to cry for America—and then change it.

Springsteen conveys compassion for the casualty, for the ordinary person who may not be articulate. His empathy is for men with "debts no honest man can pay." From his immense pride in his home town comes a homage to closed textile mills and "Main Street's whitewashed windows and vacant stores." Out of his populist patriotism comes his affection for people who feel "like a dog that's been beat too much" and his reconciling respect for his working-class father:

Daddy worked his whole life for nothing but the pain.
Now he walks up these empty rooms, looking for something to blame.

These songs are social, not political. They don't offer platforms, slogans or rhetoric. They don't imply easy remedies and they don't endorse politicians. Springsteen himself says he has not voted since 1972, and he is enrolled in no political party. . . .

Springsteen and Stallone, two messiahs of American mass culture, two muscular men—tugging this country's flag in different directions.

Sylvester Stallone, at bottom, is a faker, feeding us fantasies as therapy for our national neuroses. He is appealing to the dark side that exists in all of us, the part of us that wants to get even with everyone who has ever gotten the better of us, the part that finds it easier to understand a stereotype than an individual, the part that dreams of vengeance that never fails and never leaves an aftertaste of guilt.

Bruce Springsteen appeals to the best in all of us. His songs ask us to forgive the sinner but to remember the sin; to respect one another but to question authority; to refuse to compromise our ideals ("no retreat, no surrender"); to keep growing but to continue to love our parents and our home towns; to feel a responsibility for sharing with our countrymen who have less property and less power.

"I think what's happening now," Springsteen told one interviewer, "is people want to forget. There was Vietnam, there was Watergate, there was Iran—we were beaten, we were hustled and then we were humiliated. And I think people got a need to feel good about the country they live in. But what's happening, I think, is that need—which is a good thing—is gettin' manipulated and exploited. . . .

"One of the things that was always on my mind was to maintain connections with the people I'd grown up with and the sense of community where I came from. That's why I stayed in New Jersey. The danger of fame is in *forgetting.*"

Newfield, Jack. "Stallone vs. Springsteen." *The Compact Reader*, Second Edition, 1987. Jane E. Aaron, Editor. St. Martin's Press, pp. 191–195. ISBN: 0-312-15308-2.

Suggestions for discussion and writing:

1. Does Newfield use comparison and contrast to explain the two characters, present them as symbols, or advance an ideology?

2. Does Newfield use the block-by-block or point-by-point method?

3. Does Newfield use the first, second, or third-person form of narration in his essay?

4. Discuss the definition of "Hero."

5. Write a brief essay in which you compare and contrast the cartoon characters Donald Duck and Daffy Duck.

ANALOGY

Definition:

Analogy is a mode used to describe something in a *proportionate and comparative* manner. For example, the human heart and a mechanical pump are analogous. A writer uses analogy to establish equivalent relationships. A writer needs to incorporate classification when setting up equivalence of relationships. He can, for example, make sure that all things being compared are placed into like categories such as arms, legs, and hands, constituting body parts, as opposed to eggs, celery, and milk, comprising groceries.

Method:

Writing about the human heart and a mechanical pump in detailed point-by-point comparisons is a clear example of analogy used as a writing mode. Analogy is useful for a writer who is attempting to *develop abstract ideas by making them more easily understandable.* As a writing technique, analogy is used to serve two functions:

(1) to illustrate difficult subjects and make them easier to comprehend by comparing them to already established and well known similarities;

(2) to serve as a form of reasoning from which inferences may be drawn to establish logical conclusions.

The main point to remember is that analogy can be used to infer possible meanings based on established likenesses.

Major Points:

- Proportionate and comparative
- Develop abstract ideas
- Make ideas easily understandable
- Establish likenesses

THE SALMON INSTINCT

William Humphrey

Born in Clarksville, Texas, in 1924, William Humphrey is a writer of short stories, novels, and essays. He is an award-winning novelist with books such as Home From the Hills *(1958) and* Farther Off From Heaven *(1977). The following article is an excellent example of analogy as he describes the instinctual drive to return home.*

When James I, King of England, was asked why he was going back, after a long absence, to visit his native Scotland, he replied, "The salmon instinct."

The salmon is in his early adolescence when he leaves his native stream, impelled by an irresistible urge for something he has never known, the salt, salt sea. There he stays for the rest of his life, until he feels another prompting equally irresistible, the urge to reproduce himself. This the salmon can do only in that same stream in which he was born. And so, from distances as great as fifteen hundred miles, the old salmon heads for home.

Many things can, and do, kill the salmon on his long voyage home, but nothing can deter or detour him. Not the diseases and parasites he is prone to, not fishermen, commercial or sporting, not the highest falls. He endures them, he eludes them, he leaps them, impelled by his ardent homesickness. Though long an expatriate, he knows his nationality as a naturalized American knows his, and back to the country of his birth he goes, as though throughout all the years away he has kept his first passport. Through the pathless sea he finds his way unerringly to the river down which he came on his voyage out long ago, and past each of its tributaries, each more temptingly like the one he is seeking the nearer he gets to that special one, as towns in the same county are similar but not the same. When he gets to his, he knows it—as I, for instance, know Clarksville, and would know it even if, like the salmon, I had but one sense to lead me to it. The name given the salmon in Latin is *Salmo salar:* the fish that will leap

107

waterfalls to get back home. Some later Linnaeus of the human orders must have classed me at birth among the Humphreys: in Welsh the name means "One who loves his hearth and home."

But I began to doubt my homing instincts, to think I had wandered too far away, stayed gone too long, when, after crossing the ocean, I went back those thirty-two years later.

I had spent a few days in Dallas first, as the homecoming salmon spends a few days in the estuary to reaccustom himself to sweet water after all his years at sea before ascending to his native stream; for although that is what he now longs for, those uterine waters of his, too sudden a change from the salt is a shock to him. Dallas had always been brackish to me.

The nearer I got to Clarksville the farther from it I seemed to be. This was not where I was spawned. Strange places had usurped the names of towns I used to know. It was like what the British during World War II, fearing an invasion, had done, setting real but wrong place-names and roadsigns around the countryside so that the enemy in, say, Kent would find himself in villages belonging to Lancashire.

Gone were the spreading cottonfields I remembered, though this was the season when they should have been beginning to whiten. The few patches that remained were small and sparse, like the patches of snow lingering on in sunless spots in New England in March and April. The prairie grass that had been there before the fields were broken for cotton had reclaimed them. The woods were gone—even Sulphur Bottom, that wilderness into which my father had gone in pursuit of the fugitive gunman: grazing land now, nearly all of it. For in a move that reverses Texas history, a move totally opposite to what I knew in my childhood, one which all but turns the world upside down, which makes the sun set in the East, Red River County has ceased to be Old South and become Far West. I who for years had had to set my Northern friends straight by pointing out that I was a Southerner, not a Westerner, and that I had never seen a cowboy or for that matter a beefcow any more than they had, found myself now in that Texas of legend and the popular image which when I was a child had seemed more romantic to me than to a boy of New England precisely because it was closer to me than to him and yet still worlds away. Gone from the square were the bib overalls of my childhood when the farmers came to town on Saturday. Ranchers now, they came in high-heeled boots and rolled-brim hats, a costume that would have provoked as much surprise, and even more derision, there, in my time, as it would on Manhattan's Madison Avenue.

You can never ascend the same river twice, an early philosopher tells us. Its course, its composition are ever changing. Even so, one of its natives knows it, even one, like the salmon, who has spent most of his life away. I had been away from Clarksville since my father's death, and although ever since then I had been surprised each day to find myself alive, I was now an older man than he had lived to be. In that time much had changed in Clarksville; still, it was where I belonged.

Just as the salmon must leave home when the time comes, so he must return to round out his life. There where he was born, he dies.

Humphrey, William. "The Salmon Instinct." *Thinking in Writing*, Second Edition. Donald McQuade and Robert Atwan, Editors. Alfred A. Knopf, 1983, pp. 264–267. ISBN: 0-394-32819-1.

Suggestions for discussion and writing:

1. Why does Humphrey use analogy rather than simple statement?
2. Does Humphrey compare or contrast himself to the salmon?
3. Why does Humphrey make a distinction between farmers and ranchers?
4. Discuss Humphrey's primary subject of his analogy.
5. Write a brief essay in which you discuss whether Humphrey's use of analogy is effective or not.

TWO STATUES

Elizabeth Cady Stanton

*Elizabeth Cady Stanton (1815–1906) is best known as a
prime mover of the Women's Suffrage Movement. Along
with Susan B. Anthony and Matilda Joslyn Gage, she
wrote the comprehensive six-volume work* History of
Woman Suffrage *(1881–1886). She addressed the New
York State Legislature on February 18, 1860 regarding
equal treatment of the sexes. Her speech is an example of
the use of analogy.*

At Athens, an ancient apologue tells us, on the completion of
the temple of Minerva, a statue of the goddess was wanted to
occupy the crowning point of the edifice. Two of the greatest
artists produced what each deemed his masterpiece. One of
these figures was the size of life, admirably designed, exquis-
itely finished, softly rounded, and beautifully refined. The
other was of Amazonian stature, and so boldly chiselled that
it looked more like masonry than sculpture. The eyes of all
were attracted by the first, and turned away in contempt from
the second. That, therefore, was adopted, and the other rejected, almost with resentment, as though an insult had been
offered to a discerning public. The favored statue was accordingly borne in triumph to the place for which it was designed,
in the presence of applauding thousands, but as it receded
from their upturned eyes, all, all at once agaze upon it, the
thunders of applause unaccountably died away—a general
misgiving ran through every bosom—the mob themselves
stood like statues, as silent and as petrified, for as it slowly
went up, and up the soft expression of those chiselled features, the delicate curves and outlines of the limbs and figure,
became gradually fainter and fainter, and when at last it
reached the place for which it was intended, it was a shapeless
ball, enveloped in mist. Of course, the idol of the hour was
now clamored down as rationally as it had been cried up, and
its dishonored rival, with no good will and no good looks on

the part of the chagrined populace, was reared in its stead. As it ascended, the sharp angles faded away, the rough points became smooth, the features full of expression, the whole figure radiant with majesty and beauty. The rude hewn mass, that before had scarcely appeared to bear even the human form, assumed at once the divinity which it represented, being so perfectly proportioned to the dimensions of the building, and to the elevation on which it stood, that it seemed as though Pallas herself had alighted upon the pinnacle of the temple in person, to receive the homage of her worshippers.

The woman of the nineteenth century is the shapeless ball in the lofty position which she was designed fully and nobly to fill. The place is not too high, too large, too sacred for woman, but the type that you have chosen is far too small for it. The woman we declare unto you is the rude, misshapen, unpolished object of the successful artist. From your standpoint, you are absorbed with the defects alone. The true artist sees the harmony between the object and its destination. Man, the sculptor, has carved out his ideal, and applauding thousands welcome his success. He has made a woman that from his low stand-point looks fair and beautiful, a being without rights, or hopes, or fears but in him—neither noble, virtuous, nor independent. Where do we see, in Church or State, in school-house or at the fireside, the much talked-of moral power of woman? Like those Athenians, we have bowed down and worshiped in woman, beauty, grace, the exquisite proportions, the soft and beautifully rounded outline, her delicacy, refinement, and silent helplessness all well when she is viewed simply as an object of sight, never to rise one foot above the dust from which she sprung. But if she is to be raised up to adorn a temple, or represent a divinity—if she is to fill the niche of wife and counsellor to true and noble men, if she is to be the mother, the educator of a race of heroes or martyrs, of a Napoleon, or a Jesus—then must the type of womanhood be on a larger scale than that yet carved by man.

Stanton, Elizabeth Cady. "Two Statues." *Thinking in Writing*, Second Edition. Donald McQuade and Robert Atwan, Editors. Alfred A. Knopf, 1983, pp. 262–263. ISBN: 0-394-32819-1.

Suggestions for discussion and writing:

1. What is the connection between analogy and comparison and contrast in this essay?

2. What do the statues represent?

3. Is there a resemblance between nineteenth-century women and the statues?

4. Discuss today's women and nineteenth-century women using analogy.

5. Write an essay in which you develop an analogy between neighborhoods and countries.

'BUT A WATCH IN THE NIGHT': A SCIENTIFIC FABLE

James C. Rettie

James C. Rettie wrote this essay in 1948. Little is known of him other than the fact that he worked for the National Forest Service in suburban Philadelphia. The following essay has been reprinted numerous times by different conservation groups wishing to send a message through analogy.

Out beyond our solar system there is a planet called Copernicus. It came into existence some four or five billion years before the birth of our Earth. In due course of time it became inhabited by a race of intelligent men.

About 750 million years ago the Copernicans had developed the motion picture machine to a point well in advance of the stage that we have reached. Most of the cameras that we now use in motion picture work are geared to take twenty-four pictures per second on a continuous strip of film. When such film is run through a projector, it throws a series of images on the screen and these change with a rapidity that gives the visual impression of normal movement. If a motion is too swift for the human eye to see it in detail, it can be captured and artificially slowed down by means of the slow-motion camera. This one is geared to take many more shots per second—ninety-six or even more than that. When the slow-motion film is projected at the normal speed of twenty-four pictures per second, we can see just how the jumping horse goes over a hurdle.

What about motion that is too slow to be seen by the human eye? That problem has been solved by the use of the time-lapse camera. In this one, the shutter is geared to take only one shot per second, or one per minute, or even one per hour—depending upon the kind of movement that is being photographed. When the time-lapse film is projected at the normal speed of twenty-four pictures per second, it is possible to see a bean sprout growing up out of the ground. Time-lapse films are useful in the study of many types of motion too slow to be observed by the unaided, human eye.

The Copernicans, it seems, had time-lapse cameras some 757 million years ago and they also had superpowered telescopes that gave them a clear view of what was happening upon this Earth. They decided to make a film record of the life history of Earth and to make it on the scale of one picture per year. The photography has been in progress during the last 757 million years.

In the near future, a Copernican interstellar expedition will arrive upon our Earth and bring with it a copy of the time-lapse film. Arrangements will be made for showing the entire film in one continuous run. This will begin at midnight of New Year's eve and continue day and night without a single stop until midnight of December 31. The rate of projection will be twenty-four pictures per second. Time on the screen will thus seem to move at the rate of 24 years per second; 1,440 years per minute; 86,400 years per hour; approximately 2 million years per day; and 62 million years per month. The normal life-span of individual man will occupy about three seconds. The full period of Earth history that will be unfolded on the screen (some 757 million years) will extend from what the geologists call Pre-Cambrian times up to the present. This will, by no means, cover the full time-span of the Earth's geological history, but it will embrace the period since the advent of living organisms.

During the months of January, February and March the picture will be desolate and dreary. The shape of the land masses and the oceans will bear little or no resemblance to those that we know. The violence of geological erosion will be much in evidence. Rains will pour down on the land and promptly go booming down to the seas. There will be no clear streams anywhere except where the rains fall upon hard rock. Everywhere on the steeper ground the stream channels will be filled with boulders hurled down by rushing waters. Raging torrents and dry stream beds will keep alternating in quick succession. High mountains will seem to melt like so much butter in the sun. The shifting of land into the seas, later to be thrust up as new mountains, will be going on at a grand scale.

Early in April there will be some indication of the presence of single-celled living organisms in some of the warmer and sheltered coastal waters. By the end of the month it will be noticed that some of these organisms have become multicellular. A few of them, including the Trilobites, will be encased in hard shells.

Toward the end of May, the first vertebrates will appear, but they will still be aquatic creatures. In June about 60 percent of the land area that we know as North America will be under water. One broad channel will occupy the space where the Rocky Mountains now stand. Great deposits of limestone will be forming under some of the shallower seas. Oil and gas deposits will be in process of formation— also under shallow seas. On land there will still be no sign of vegetation. Erosion will be rampant, tearing loose particles and chunks of rock and grinding them into sand and silt to be spewed out by the streams into bays and estuaries.

About the middle of July the first land plants will appear and take up the tremendous job of soil building. Slowly, very slowly, the mat of vegetation will spread, always battling for its life against the power of erosion. Almost foot by foot, the plant life will advance, lacing down with its root structures whatever pulverized rock material it can find. Leaves and stems will be giving added protection against the loss of the soil foothold. The increasing vegetation will pave the way for the land animals that will live upon it.

Early in August the seas will be teeming with fish. This will be what geologists call the Devonian period. Some of the races of these fish will be breathing by means of lung tissue instead of through gill tissues. Before the month is over, some of the lung fish will go ashore and take on a crude lizard-like appearance. Here are the first amphibians.

In early September the insects will put in their appearance. Some will look like huge dragon flies and will have a wingspread of 24 inches. Large portions of the land masses will now be covered with heavy vegetation that will include the primitive spore-propagating trees. Layer upon layer of this plant growth will build up, later to appear as the coal deposits. About the middle of this month, there will be evidence of the first seed-bearing plants and the first reptiles. Heretofore, the land animals will have been amphibians that could reproduce their kind only by depositing a soft egg mass in quiet waters. The reptiles will be shown to be freed from the aquatic bond because they can reproduce by means of a shelled egg in which the embryo and its nurturing liquids are sealed in and thus protected from destructive evaporation. Before September is over, the first dinosaurs will be seen—creatures destined to dominate the animal realm for about 140 million years and then to disappear.

In October there will be series of mountain uplifts along what is now the eastern coast of the United States. A creature with feathered limbs—half bird and half reptile in appearance—will take itself into the air. Some small and rather unpretentious animals will be seen to bring forth their young in a form that is miniature replica of the parents and to feed these young on milk secreted by mammary glands in the female parent. The emergence of this mammalian form of animal life will be recognized as one of the great events in geologic time. October will also witness the high water mark of the dinosaurs—creatures ranging in size from that of the modern goat to monsters like Brontosaurus that weighed some 40 tons. Most of them will be placid vegetarians, but a few will be hideous-looking carnivores, like Allosaurus and Tyrannosaurus. Some of the herbivorous dinosaurs will be clad in bony armor for protection against their flesh-eating comrades.

November will bring pictures of a sea extending from the Gulf of Mexico to the Arctic in space now occupied by the Rocky Mountains. A few of the reptiles will take to the air on bat-like wings. One of these, called Pteranodon, will have a wingspread of 15 feet. There will be a rapid development of the modern flowering plants, modern trees, and modern insects. The dinosaurs will disappear. Toward the end of the month there will be a tremendous land disturbance in which the Rocky Mountains will rise out of the sea to assume a dominating place in the North American landscape.

As the picture runs on into December, it will show the mammals in command of the animal life. Seed-bearing trees and grasses will have covered most of the land with a heavy mantle of vegetation. Only the areas newly thrust up from the sea will be barren. Most of the streams will be crystal clear. The turmoil of geologic erosion will be confined to localized areas. About December 25 will begin the cutting of the Grand Canyon of the Colorado River. Grinding down through layer after layer of sedimentary strata, this stream will finally expose deposits laid down in Pre-Cambrian times. Thus in the walls of that canyon will appear geological formations dating from recent times to the period when the Earth had no living organisms upon it.

The picture will run on through the latter days of December and even up to its final day with still no sign of mankind. The spectators will become alarmed in the fear that man has somehow been left out. But not so; sometime about noon on December 31 (one million years ago) will appear a stooped, massive creature of man-like proportions. This will be Pithecanthropus, the Java ape man. For tools and weapons he will have nothing but crude stone and wooden clubs. His children will live a precarious existence threatened on the one side by hostile animals and on the other by tremendous climatic changes. Ice sheets—in places 4000 feet deep—will form in the northern parts of North America and Eurasia. Four times this glacial ice will push southward to cover half the continents. With each advance the plant and animal life will be swept under or pushed southward. With each recession of the ice, life will struggle to reestablish itself in the wake of the retreating glaciers. The wooly mammoth, the musk ox, and the caribou all will fight to maintain themselves near the ice line. Sometimes they will be caught and put into cold storage—skin, flesh, blood, bones and all.

The picture will run on through supper time with still very little evidence of man's presence on the Earth. It will be about 11 o'clock when Neanderthal man appears. Another half hour will go by before the appearance of Cro-Magnon man living in caves and painting crude animal pictures on the walls of his dwelling. Fifteen minutes more will bring Neolithic man, knowing how to chip stone and thus produce sharp cutting edges for spears and tools. In a few minutes more it will appear that man has domesticated the dog, the sheep and, possibly, other animals. He will then begin the use of milk. He will also learn the arts of basket weaving and the making of pottery and dugout canoes.

The dawn of civilization will not come until about five or six minutes before the end of the picture. The story of the

Egyptians, the Babylonians, the Greeks, and the Romans will unroll during the fourth, the third and the second minute before the end. At 58 minutes and 43 seconds past 11:00 P.M. (just 1 minute and 17 seconds before the end) will come the beginning of the Christian era. Columbus will discover the new world 20 seconds before the end. The Declaration of Independence will be signed just 7 seconds before the final curtain comes down.

In those few moments of geologic time will be the story of all that has happened since we became a nation. And what a story it will be! A human swarm will sweep across the face of the continent and take it away from the primitive red men. They will change it far more radically than it has ever been changed before in a comparable time. The great virgin forests will be seen going down before ax and fire. The soil, covered for aeons by its protective mantle of trees and grasses, will be laid bare to the ravages of water and wind erosion. Streams that had been flowing clear will, once again, take up a load of silt and push it toward the seas. Humus and mineral salts, both vital elements of productive soil, will be seen to vanish at a terrifying rate. The railroads and highways and cities that will spring up may divert attention, but they cannot cover up the blight of man's recent activities. In great sections of Asia, it will be seen that man must utilize cow dung and every scrap of available straw or grass for fuel to cook his food. The forests that once provided wood for this purpose will be gone without a trace. The use of these agricultural wastes for fuel, in place of returning them to the land, will be leading to increasing soil impoverishment. Here and there will be seen a dust storm darkening the landscape over an area a thousand miles across. Man-creatures will be shown counting their wealth in terms of bits of printed paper representing other bits of a scarce but comparatively useless yellow metal that is kept buried in strong vaults. Meanwhile, the soil, the only real wealth that can keep mankind alive on the face of this Earth, is savagely being cut loose from its ancient moorings and washed into the seven seas.

We have just arrived upon this Earth. How long will we stay?

Rettie, James C. "But a Watch in the Night: A Scientific Fable." *The Compact Reader*, Second Edition. Jane E. Aaron, Editor. St. Martin's Press, 1987, pp. 224–229. ISBN: 0-312-15308-2.

Suggestions for discussion and writing:

1. What is Rettie's purpose for writing the essay?
2. What is the main subject?
3. Does Rettie use classification and division?
4. Discuss Rettie's shift from the objective third-person to the subjective first-person.
5. Write an analogy explaining the astrological term "light-years."

DEFINITION

Definition:

Definition is used to *explain* what something is and to *set limits* upon that explanation. Formal definition is generally used by a writer to name an object or concept to be defined, place it in a class, and to qualify it from other members of that class. Many times a writer and an audience may not have the same concept of what a given term may mean. It is the responsibility of the writer to establish the universe of discourse by declaring what the term will mean in the context of the essay. The term pipe, for example, can have various meanings. If the intent of the writer is to have the audience understand that pipe refers to the type that one smokes with tobacco, then it is necessary to establish that definition immediately so that there will not be any confusion regarding the meaning of the word in the essay.

The Method:

In its simplest form, a definition is used as an explanation of the meaning of a word or an idea. When employing definition as a mode, a writer has several choices regarding forms of definition. There is the *short form* where the writer uses a *synonym,* which is a familiar word or phrase that has a similar meaning as the term being described. The internal combustion machine, for example, can be defined simply as a car. In this case the term "car" stands for the "internal combustion machine." Sometimes the writer may wish to use an *antonym,* which is a word or phrase that has an opposite meaning, to define a word or idea through contrast. For example, a gentle man can be defined as "he was a lamb, rather than a wolf, in his behavior." A *formal standard dictionary definition* is also useful as a short form when used to set forth a mutually acceptable definition for the writer and the reader. This type of definition is known as formal, and the writer uses classification to define. He first assigns the word a class to which it belongs, then proceeds to describe the particular characteristics that distinguish it from other members of that class. All of these are *short definitions.*

A writer can also use an *extended definition.* When employing this form, the writer includes examples, connotations, denotations, descriptions, comparisons, and contrasts. The extended definition is used by the writer so that he may explain lengthy and complex ideas through the various techniques found in definition. The most important thing for the author to remember is to set the limits as to what the idea means to both the writer and the reader. A pig, for example, can mean different things to many people. Following a formal definition which is denotative, a pig is an animal of a given class. The connotation that most people assign a pig is usually negative, and considered in terms of filth. A person who does not clean his room may often be termed a pig. A pig makes a great deal of noise when eating and usually places its snout deep into the trough. A person with poor eating habits or bad table manners may also be referred to as a pig. To clarify an extended definition, a writer ought to first establish a formal definition, whether denotative or connotative, because this removes any ambiguity that may exist in terms of the meaning of the word. Next, he should offer an antonym or synonym as a means for clarifying the word or idea. After that, the writer should present two or three examples to demonstrate the similarities of the word or idea to be conveyed. To solidify the definition, the writer ought to offer some comparisons and contrasts to define, beyond a doubt, what it is that he wishes to convey.

Major Points:
- Explain
- Set limits
- Use short forms such as synonyms, antonyms, and formal definitions
- Use extended forms such as comparison, contrast, and examples

THE HOLOCAUST

Bruno Bettelheim

Bruno Bettelheim is best known as a child psychologist and psychiatrist. He worked at Chicago University as a professor of education, psychology, and psychiatry, and produced many important books including The Uses of Enchantment: The Meaning and Importance of Fairy Tales *(1976) and* On Learning to Read: The Child's Fascination with Meaning *(1982). A survivor of the Holocaust who spent time in Buchenwald and Dachau concentration camps, Bettelheim examines the term "Holocaust" in his essay which is an analytical classic of definition as a means to understanding.*

To begin with, it was not the hapless victims of the Nazis who named their incomprehensible and totally unmasterable fate the "holocaust. "It was the Americans who applied this artificial and highly technical term to the Nazi extermination of the European Jews. But while the event when named as mass murder most foul evokes the most immediate, most powerful revulsion, when it is designated by a rare technical term, we must first in our minds translate it back into emotionally meaningful language. Using technical or specially created terms instead of words from our common vocabulary is one of the best-known and most widely used distancing devices, separating the intellectual from the emotional experience. Talking about "the holocaust" permits us to manage it intellectually where the raw facts, when given their ordinary names, would overwhelm us emotionally—because it was catastrophe beyond comprehension, beyond the limits of our imagination, unless we force ourselves against our desire to extend it to encompass these terrible events.

This linguistic circumlocution began while it all was only in the planning stage. Even the Nazis—usually given to grossness in language and action—shied away from facing openly what they were up to and called this vile mass murder "the final solution of the Jewish problem." After all, solving a problem can be made to appear like an honorable enterprise, as long as we are not forced to recognize that the solution we are about to embark on consists of the completely unprovoked, vicious murder of millions of helpless men, women, and children. The Nuremberg judges of these Nazi criminals followed their example of circumlocution by coining a neologism out of one Greek and one Latin root: genocide. These artificially created technical terms fail to connect with our strongest feelings. The horror of murder is part of our most common human heritage. From earliest infancy on, it arouses violent abhorrence in us. Therefore in whatever form it appears we should give such an act its true designation and not hide it behind polite, erudite terms created out of classical words.

To call this vile mass murder "the holocaust" is not to give it a special name emphasizing its uniqueness which would permit, over time, the word becoming invested with feelings germane to the event it refers to. The correct definition of "holocaust" is "burnt offering." As such, it is part of the language of the psalmist, a meaningful word to all who have some acquaintance with the Bible, full of the richest emotional connotations. By using the term "holocaust," entirely false associations are established through conscious and unconscious connotations between the most vicious of mass murders and ancient rituals of a deeply religious nature.

Using a word with such strong unconscious religious connotations when speaking of the murder of millions of Jews robs the victims of this abominable mass murder of the only thing left to them: their uniqueness. Calling the most callous, most brutal, most horrid, most heinous mass murder a burnt offering is a sacrilege, a profanation of God and man.

Martyrdom is part of our religious heritage. A martyr, burned at the stake, is a burnt offering to his god. And it is true that after the Jews were asphyxiated, the victims' corpses were burned. But I believe we fool ourselves if we think we are honoring the victims of systematic murder by using this term, which has the highest moral connotations. By doing so, we connect for our own psychological reasons what happened in the extermination camps with historical events we deeply regret, but also greatly admire. We do so because this makes it easier for us to cope; only in doing so we cope with our distorted image of what happened, not with the events the way they did happen.

By calling the victims of the Nazis "martyrs," we falsify their fate. The true meaning of "martyr" is: "one who voluntarily undergoes the penalty of death for refusing to renounce his faith" *(Oxford English Dictionary)*. The Nazis made sure that nobody could mistakenly think that their victims were murdered for their religious beliefs. Renouncing their faith would have saved none of them. Those who had converted to Christianity were gassed, as were those who were atheists, and those who were deeply religious Jews. They did not die for any conviction, and certainly not out of choice.

Millions of Jews were systematically slaughtered, as were untold other "undesirables," not for any convictions of theirs, but only because they stood in the way of the realization of an illusion. They neither died for their convictions, nor were they slaughtered because of their convictions, but only in consequence of the Nazis' delusional belief about what was required to protect the purity of their assumed superior racial endowment, and what they thought necessary to guarantee them the living space they believed they needed and were entitled to. Thus while these millions were slaughtered for an idea, they did not die for one.

Millions—men, women, and children—were processed after they had been utterly brutalized, their humanity destroyed, their clothes torn from their bodies. Naked, they were sorted into those who were destined to be murdered immediately, and those others who had a short-term usefulness as slave labor. But after a brief interval they, too, were to be herded into the same gas chambers into which the others were immediately piled, there to be asphyxiated so that, in their last moments, they could not prevent themselves from fighting each other in vain for a last breath of air.

To call these most wretched victims of a murderous delusion, of destructive drives run rampant, martyrs or a burnt offering is a distortion invented for our comfort, small as it may be. It pretends that this most vicious of mass murders had some deeper meaning; that in some fashion the victims either offered themselves or at least became sacrifices to a higher cause. It robs them of the last recognition which could be theirs, denies them the last dignity we could accord them:

to face and accept what their death was all about, not embellishing it for the small psychological relief this may give us.

We could feel so much better if the victims had acted out of choice. For our emotional relief, therefore, we dwell on the tiny minority who did exercise some choice: the resistance fighters of the Warsaw ghetto, for example, and others like them. We are ready to overlook the fact that these people fought back only at a time when everything was lost, when the overwhelming majority of those who had been forced into the ghettos had already been exterminated without resisting. Certainly those few who finally fought for their survival and their convictions, risking and losing their lives in doing so, deserve our admiration; their deeds give us a moral lift. But the more we dwell on these few, the more unfair are we to the memory of the millions who were slaughtered—who gave in, did not fight back—because we deny them the only thing which up to the very end remained uniquely their own: their fate.

Bettelheim, Bruno. "The Holocaust." *Thinking in Writing*, Second Edition. Donald McQuade and Robert Atwan, Editors. Alfred A. Knopf, 1983, pp. 130–133. ISBN: 0-394-32819-1.

Suggestions for discussion and writing:

1. Does Bettelheim use the word "genocide" to protect the reader from the severity of the action described?
2. Are Bettelheim's word choices appropriate for his purpose?
3. Does a writer use definition to set limits?
4. Discuss the use of words as tools to manipulate.
5. Write an essay in which you discuss some group that has redefined itself.

GRANDPARENTS

Nancy Pritts Merril

Nancy Pritts Merril, a recent college graduate, wrote this essay while still a student. It is an example of extended definition. Merril helps the reader understand feelings and attitudes through the use of definition.

Of all family members, grandparents are probably the least appreciated. They are just people who are always around. They make a fuss over the children in the family, brag to their friends about the accomplishments of this child or that child, and show countless pictures of new babies. Grandfathers can fix anything, and grandmothers always have homemade cookies around. When you are small, it's fun to stay with your grandparents because they always let you do things you can't do at home, and of course they buy you things. They are always available to babysit because they don't go out much and actually prefer to see their grandchildren. They are usually good for a small loan now and then that doesn't need to be paid back because they turn it into a gift. You respectfully listen to their advice but don't follow it because they are old and don't understand how things are in this day and age. You thank them politely for what they do for you, and then don't call or visit them until you need something else. And of course you never tell them how dear they are to you because they know how you feel about them anyway. Then all of a sudden, they are no longer there to do the things that only grandparents do, and you find yourself wishing that you had told them what they meant to you as people and not just as grandparents.

Merril, Nancy Pritts. "Grandparents." *Patterns Plus,* Third Edition. Mary Lou Conlin, Editor. Houghton Mifflin Company, 1990, p. 310. ISBN: 0-395-51691-9.

Suggestions for discussion and writing:

1. How does Merril define grandparents?
2. What is the main idea of Merril's essay?
3. What is Merril's point in the last sentence?
4. Discuss a particular word, looking to give it the fullest possible definition.
5. Write an essay in which you define guilt.

I LOVE YOU

Robert C. Solomon

Robert C. Solomon, a freelance writer, takes an almost indefinable phrase, and presents it clearly and expressively.

"I love you" does not always have the same meaning, and this, too, should tell us something about the elusive nature of love. The first time it is always a surprise, an invasion, an aggressive act, but once said, "I love you" can only be repeated. It is unthinkable that it should not be said again, and again, and again. When one has not said it for a while, this may itself precipitate a crisis. ("Now why haven't you said that in all of these months!") On the other hand, "I love you" can also serve as a threat ("Don't push me on this; you might lose me"), emotional blackmail ("I've said it, now you have to respond in kind"), a warning ("It's only because I love you that I'm willing to put up with this"), an apology ("I could not possibly have meant what I have said to you, *to you* of all people"). It can be an instrument—more effective than the loudest noise—to interrupt a dull or painful conversation. It can be a cry, a plea, a verbal flag ("Pay attention to me!") or it can be an excuse ("It's only because I love you. . ."). It can be a disguise ("I love you," he whispered, looking awkwardly askance at the open door.). It can be an attack ("How can you do this to me?") or even an end ("So that's that. With regrets, good-bye."). If this single phrase has so many meanings, how varied and variable must be the emotion.

Solomon, Robert. C. "I Love You." *Patterns Plus*, Third Edition. Mary Lou Conlin, Editor. Houghton Mifflin Company, 1990, p. 306. ISBN: 0-395-51691-9.

Suggestions for discussion and writing:

1. Does Solomon use emotion in his essay?
2. What is the basis for Solomon's essay?
3. How does Solomon use example to make his point?
4. Discuss dating in terms of love.
5. Write an essay about Valentine's Day.

CAUSE AND EFFECT

Definition:

When using cause and effect as a mode, the writer incorporates two complementary concepts. The writer employs *cause* to refer to *what makes things happen,* and *effect* to refer to the results or *what does happen.* A cause is used to presuppose one or more effects, and an effect always has one or more results. Cause and effect essays are usually designed to be *informative or persuasive.* A writer using the informative approach will focus upon causal relationships in an objective manner, presenting them as facts. When employing cause and effect as persuasive writing, the author will generally investigate causal relationships so as to persuade the audience to a particular point of view or toward some form of action.

Method:

When employing cause and effect, a writer attempts to explain or persuade. He often discusses why something happened or what its outcome might be. When attempting to use cause and effect the writer should discuss an experience or situation, and then specifically identify the *immediate cause* and its subsequent connections. Causes and effects often occur in links, otherwise known singularly as a causal chain. The writer forges each link in order to contribute something to the resultant effect of the next. Immediate causes are those that occur nearest an event such as the closing of the Jello plant in Leroy, N.Y. which led to the loss of jobs for the local residents. There are also *remote causes* such as the declining market for the Jello Company in Western New York as the inhabitants moved to the newly prosperous Southern city, Atlanta, Georgia, where Jello sales increased accordingly.

It is important to distinguish the relative *significance* of events when analyzing cause and effect by identifying which events are *major* and which are *minor.* The Jello plant may have closed because of lagging sales, a major event, but it also may have closed because of a prohibitive cost for replacing antiquated equipment, a minor, but important aspect of the cause and effect analysis.

129

Cause and effect events are complex, and a writer needs to exercise care when explaining them. He must be especially careful not to attribute coincidence to cause. The Jello plant, for example, may have been closed, and shortly thereafter vandalized. Some may attribute that vandalism to disgruntled ex-employees, however, since there is neither direct nor circumstantial evidence to substantiate such a claim, then the vandalism properly belongs to the category of coincidence.

Oversimplification is another area where a writer needs to exercise care. There are both *single and multiple cause effects* that need to be distinguished when using cause and effect as a mode:

(1) a single cause must occur in order for an effect to happen. A single cause leading to a single effect is the easiest model to understand;

(2) a multiple cause is one in which a single cause produces multiple effects. A multiple cause is recognizable by the consequences.

For example, a car has defective brakes and crashes into a building. The single cause of the crash is mechanical and the effect is the crash. As a result of the crash, a fire breaks out and people are killed and property damage is high. The multiple cause is mechanical, and the effects are the crash, fire, deaths, and property loss:

Single cause — defective brakes = crash

Multiple causes — defective brakes = crash

= fire

= deaths

= property loss

A writer can clarify the problem of oversimplification by thinking of *single cause effects and multiple cause effects.*

Major Points:

- Cause = what makes things happen
- Effect = what does happen
- Immediate and remote causes
- Distinguish major and minor events
- Distinguish single and multiple cause effects
- Cause and Effect, as a mode, is informative or persuasive

THE NEXT ICE AGE

Sir Frederick Hoyle

Born in Yorkshire, England, in 1915, Hoyle is one of England's most respected mathematicians and writers. A graduate of Cambridge University, he has earned numerous academic honors, including knighthood in 1972. He is the author of The Nature of the Universe *(1950),* Man and Materialism *(1955), and* Of Men and Galaxies *(1966), as well as a large number of short stories and essays.*

More than three-quarters of all the ice in the world is in the southern polar continent of Antarctica, a conveniently distant place. Most of the rest of the world's ice lies in Greenland, also a remote place. So we are accustomed to thinking of the heavily populated lands of the Earth as being ice-free, except for the minute smears of the stuff we encounter in winter.

The Stone Age people who executed the magnificent cave paintings to be seen in southwest France and Spain did not enjoy such a pleasant situation. Twenty thousand years ago an ice sheet comparable to the one now in Greenland lay across Scandinavia. It had extensions reaching into Russia, Germany, and Britain. Another ice sheet of polar dimensions lay across the heartland of Canada, and its extensions reached beyond Chicago.

Nor was the grim situation of 20,000 years ago confined to the northern temperate latitudes. That ice age extended fingers even into the tropics. Substantial glaciers appeared on high tropical mountains such as those in Hawaii.

In the luxury of our present ice-free state we are apt to think that the ice age is over. But all the evidence is that the piling of vast quantities of ice onto the northern temperate latitudes (a belt of land running from the U.S.S.R. through Western Europe to Canada and the U.S.) has scarcely begun. To understand the overwhelming threat the future has in store for mankind, let us go back several tens of millions of years.

It is well known that the continents of the Earth are not in fixed positions; they drift about slowly in characteristic periods of 50 to 100 million years. About 40 million years ago the continent of Antarctica moved toward the South Pole. This caused the first glaciers there, and about 20 million years ago Antarctica was substantially ice covered.

A sinister process then set in, with its origin in the remarkable inability of the direct rays of the sun to melt either snow or ice. Most sunshine is reflected by snow, while it penetrates ice so deeply and diffusely that it has little melting effect at its surface. The sun does nothing directly to Antarctic ice, which would accumulate indefinitely from repeated snowfalls if icebergs did not break away into the sea at the outer edges of the ice sheet.

By about 20 million years ago a balance between the gain of new ice and the loss of old ice had been set up. The icebergs chilled the surrounding salty water. If this cooled water had remained at the ocean surface no harm would have been done. Despite its inability to melt ice and snow, sunlight is highly effective at warming the surface layers of the ocean, and would soon have resupplied the heat lost to the icebergs. This did not happen, however, because the dense, cool water sank from the surface to the ocean depths and the deep basins began to fill with water that was literally ice-cold.

This process eventually changed the warm world ocean of 50 million years ago into today's overwhelmingly ice-cold world ocean—with a thin skin of warmer water at its surface. Only this thin warm skin protects us from the next ice age.

As the chilling of the deep ocean occurred slowly and inexorably the Earth's climate worsened. By about 10 million years ago glaciers had appeared in Alaska. The first major intrusion of ice onto the lands of the northern temperate belt occurred about two million years ago. From time to time the ice would melt and for a while the land would be ice-free. Then the ice would come, again and again.

The ice-age periods became progressively longer than the intervening interglacials. In the past million years the situation has worsened, until the average interglacial period has now shrunk to no more than 10,000 years. Since this is just the length of time since the present warm interglacial period began, our ration of ice-free conditions is over. The next ice age is already due.

A sequence of ice ages continues for as long as the continent in question resides at the pole in question. Our present sequence of ice ages will therefore continue for as long as the continent of Antarctica remains at the South Pole, which will probably be for several more tens of millions of years. The conclusion is that the present sequence of ice ages has scarcely begun. There are hundreds of ice ages still to come.

Why should there be an alternating sequence of ice ages and interglacials? At present snow lies during the winter over most of the northern temperate region. Instead of accumulating year by year into continental ice sheets, it melts each spring and summer. This is the essence of the interglacial condition. We are ice-free now, not because of a lack of snowfall but because of the spring thaw.

Melting comes from warmth in the air. Unlike the sun's direct rays, the longer-wave heat radiation generated by warm air is absorbed in snow or ice, which therefore melts almost immediately, thin surface layer after thin surface layer. The process is highly efficient and, given a sufficient supply of warm air, a whole winter's snow melts in a few days. Thus winter snow stays until warm air comes, and almost in a flash it is gone.

Where does the warm air get its heat? Mostly from the surface layer of warm ocean water that overlies the mass of ice-cold deeper water. Remove the surface layer of warm ocean water and there would then be no warm air. The snows of winter would not melt, ice sheets would begin to build, and the next ice age would have arrived.

The important surface layer of warm ocean water stores about ten times more heat than is required by the air and the land each year, a ten-to-one margin of safety. That is enough to have prevented the next ice age for 10,000 years, but not sufficient to withstand every kind of accident. The finest particles of ash thrown into the air by the recent eruption of the Mount St. Helens volcano will take about ten years to settle down to ground level. Fine particles of any electrically insulating material reflect sunlight back into space and so reduce the amount available to heat the ocean surface. The Mount St. Helens volcanic eruption was not remotely big enough to have produced such a reflecting layer around the Earth.

In 1815 Mount Tambora in the Dutch East Indies produced an explosion that threw a sufficient quantity of fine ash into the high atmosphere to have a noticeable effect on the Northern Hemisphere summer of 1816. It was a summer of agricultural disaster in New England, the coldest on record at places as widely separated as New Haven and Geneva.

As an astronomer, I prefer to consider the possibility of a similar but much more violent effect triggered from outside the Earth: the impact of a giant meteorite. There is no question that giant meteorites, half a mile long or more, must hit the Earth from time to time, and such collisions must throw a vast quantity of debris into the atmosphere.

The most notable meteoritic event of modern times occurred in July, 1908. Miss K. Stephens wrote to *The Times* from Godman-chester about a strange light she had seen in the midnight sky, commenting that "it would be interesting if anyone could explain the cause." It was not until 1927 that even the point of impact of the meteorite was discovered, by an expedition that penetrated to the Tunguska River region in Siberia. An enormous area of devastation was found, almost twice that caused by Mount St. Helens, showing that a comparatively minor meteoritic collision can be far more destructive than the explosion of a volcano.

Once in every 5,000 to 10,000 years a meteoritic collision occurs which projects sufficient fine dust into the high atmosphere to make the Earth into a temporarily reflective planet. The resulting cutoff of sunlight robs the surface waters of the terrestrial ocean of their protective store of heat, and the air that blows over the land from the sea is then no longer warm enough to melt the snows of winter.

How long will the snow accumulate? Within two or three decades at most, all the fine dust will have settled to the Earth's surface under gravity and sunlight will no longer be reflected back into space. Warm summer air will blow again over the land, and within only a further year or two the accumulated snows will be melted into lakes, streams, and rivers. Admittedly, there would have been a number of very bad years, enough to throw human society into a crisis beside which the multitudinous troubles which now dog our daily lives would seem like pinpricks. But after half a century things would be back to normal—seemingly.

This apparent loophole in what had seemed an inexorable line of reasoning troubled me for a long time until the day I chanced on a description of the following simple experiment: If air that has not been thoroughly dried, that contains a number of very small water drops, is cooled progressively in a chamber, the droplets do not solidify into ice crystals as their temperature falls below the normal freezing point, but remain as a supercooled liquid down to a remarkably low temperature, close to -40°C, when at last the liquid water goes into ice.

If a beam of light passes through the chamber, and if one looks at it from a direction at right angles to the beam, the chamber appears dark so long as the droplets stay liquid. Their transition to ice is signaled by a sudden radiance from the interior of the chamber. This means that whereas liquid droplets transmit light beams, ice crystals scatter them.

Even in the driest desert regions of the Earth there is always more than sufficient water in the air, if it is condensed from vapor into fine crystals of ice, to produce an almost perfectly reflective blanket. Does this happen anywhere? It does, particularly in the polar regions. The ice crystals are known to polar explorers as "diamond dust," a name that illustrates their brilliant reflective properties. Diamond dust is responsible for a bewildering range of optical effects halos, mock suns, arcs, coronas, and iridescent clouds.

Why does diamond dust not form everywhere? Because except in the polar regions, water droplets in the atmosphere are kept above the critical temperature, near -40°C, at which they would be transformed into ice. What prevents the temperature of water droplets from falling to -40°C throughout much of the high atmosphere is heat from the oceans. Reduce the heat supplied by the oceans to the air by about 25 per cent and diamond dust would form, not just in the polar regions but over much of the Earth.

But this is exactly what would happen in the situation I have described: fine particles thrown up into the high atmosphere, either by an enormous volcano or by the collision of a giant meteorite, would cool the surface of the ocean and the ability of the ocean to supply heat to the air would be significantly reduced. Diamond dust would create an additional particle blanket around the Earth that would stay long after the first particles had fallen to ground level under gravity, and the diamond dust would then take over the job of reflecting sunlight, and so keep the ocean cool indefinitely.

Clearly, there are two distinct self-maintaining cycles of the world climate. If the surface layer of the ocean is warm, as it is at present, enough heat passes from the ocean to the air to prevent diamond dust forming, except in polar regions. Sunlight comes through to the ocean and keeps the surface warm. This is the first cycle.

The second goes exactly the opposite way. If the surface of the ocean is cool, insufficient heat goes into the air to prevent diamond dust forming. Significantly more sunlight is then reflected back into space and the surface of the ocean remains cool.

Both the first and second cycles are logically consistent. If the Earth happens to be in either of them it tends to stay in that cycle, unless a catastrophic incident causes a sudden jump from the one cycle to the other. Indeed, the two cycles are exactly those I have described as interglacials and ice ages, and the interlaced sequence of ice ages and the interglacials arises because of such catastrophic events as collisions of the Earth with giant meteorites or explosions of volcanoes.

Ice ages have exceedingly abrupt terminations. Something about the end of the last ice age took the mammoths by surprise. Along with the mastodon and woolly rhinoceros, they became extinct. Complete mammoths with surprisingly little degeneration have been recovered from present-day ice in Siberia. Either they died of hypothermia caused by freezing rain, or they blundered into bogs and pools of exceedingly cold water formed from melting permafrost.

When one considers the effect on mammoths of sudden heat from a brassy sky caused by the absorbent particles thrown up by an iron meteorite, all the evidence falls into place. The frozen ground would soften and the mammoths would flounder. Frozen pools and lakes would partially melt. In the conditions of poor visibility, the mammoths and other animals would be likely to blunder to their deaths in the icy bogs.

The progression of catastrophic events controls the sequence of ice ages and interglacial periods. The grim aspect of this is that because of the suddenness of the catastrophic events, switches back and forth between interglacial cycles and ice-age cycles occur swiftly, in timespans of a few decades at most.

One may derive some consolation from the possibility that the switch to the next ice age may still be several thousand years into the future. On the other hand, the switch could have occurred in 1908, if the giant meteorite whose light was seen by Miss K. Stephens had happened to be larger. The switch could occur tomorrow, and if it were to do so there is no human being, young or old, who would escape its appalling consequences.

Hoyle, Frederick Sir. "The Next Ice Age." *Thnking in Writing*, Second Edition. Donald McQuade and Robert Atwan, Editors. Alfred A. Knopf, 1983, pp. 409–415. ISBN: 0-394-32819-1.

Suggestions for discussion and writing:

1. How does Hoyle use language to establish cause and effect?
2. Is Hoyle's essay too rigidly constructed in terms of causal occurrences?
3. How does Hoyle use sequence to advance his argument?
4. Discuss the original cause of the universe.
5. Write an essay in which you argue the remote causes of the closing of American automobile plants.

WOMEN IN SCIENCE

K. C. Cole

K.C. Cole is an essayist and journalist who was born in 1946 in Detroit, Michigan. After graduation from Columbia University she embarked upon a career in journalism and has held many important posts with publication companies such as Newsday and Saturday Review. Cole has written several books, including Colors and Images and Things that Glow in the Dark *(1980),* Between the Lines *(1982), and* Sympathetic Vibrations: Physics as a Way of Life *(1984). The following essay was published in* The New York Times *in 1981.*

I know few other women who do what I do. What I do is write about science, mainly physics. And to do that, I spend a lot of time reading about science, talking to scientists and struggling to understand physics. In fact, most of the women (and men) I know think me quite queer for actually liking physics. "How can you write about that stuff" they ask, always somewhat askance. "I could never understand that in a million years." Or more simply, "I hate science."

I didn't realize what an odd creature a woman interested in physics was until a few years ago when a science magazine sent me to Johns Hopkins University in Baltimore for a conference on an electrical phenomenon known as the Hall effect. We sat in a huge lecture hall and listened as physicists talked about things engineers didn't understand, and engineers talked about things physicists didn't understand. What I didn't understand was why, out of several hundred young students of physics and engineering in the room, less than a handful were women.

Sometime later, I found myself at the California Institute of Technology reporting on the search for the origins of the universe. I interviewed physicist after physicist, man after man. I asked one young administrator why none of the physicists were women. And he answered: "I don't know, but I suppose it must be something innate. My seven-year-old daughter doesn't seem to be much interested in science."

It was with that experience fresh in my mind that I attended a conference in Cambridge, Mass., on science literacy, or rather the worrisome lack of it in this country today. We three women—a science teacher, a young chemist and myself—sat surrounded by a company of august men. The chemist, I think, first tentatively raised the issue of science illiteracy in women. It seemed like an obvious point. After all, everyone had agreed over and over again that scientific knowledge these days was a key factor in economic power. But as soon as she made the point, it became clear that we women had committed a grievous social error. Our genders were suddenly showing; we had interrupted the serious talk with a subject unforgivably silly.

For the first time, I stopped being puzzled about why there weren't any women in science and began to be angry. Because if science is a search for answers to fundamental questions then it hardly seems frivolous to find out why women are excluded. Never mind the economic consequences.

A lot of the reasons women are excluded are spelled out by the Massachusetts Institute of Technology experimental physicist Vera Kistiakowsky in a recent article in *Physics Today* called "Women in Physics: Unnecessary, Injurious and Out of Place?" The title was taken from a nineteenth-century essay written in opposition to the appointment of a female mathematician to a professorship at the University of Stockholm. "As decidedly as two and two make four," a woman in mathematics is a "monstrosity," concluded the writer of the essay.

Dr. Kistiakowsky went on to discuss the factors that make women in science today, if not monstrosities, at least oddities. Contrary to much popular opinion, one of those is *not* an innate difference in the scientific ability of boys and girls. But early conditioning does play a stubborn and subtle role. A recent *Nova* program, "The Pinks and the Blues," documented how girls and boys are treated differently from birth—the boys always encouraged in more physical kinds of play, more active explorations of their environments. Sheila Tobias, in her book, *Math Anxiety*, showed how the games boys play help them to develop an intuitive understanding of speed, motion and mass.

The main sorting out of the girls from the boys in science seems to happen in junior high school. As a friend who teaches in a science museum said, "By the time we get to electricity, the boys already have had some experience with it. But it's unfamiliar to the girls." Science books draw on boys' experiences. "The examples are all about throwing a baseball at such and such a speed," said my stepdaughter, who barely escaped being a science drop-out.

The most obvious reason there are not many more women in science is that women are discriminated against as a class, in promotions, salaries and hirings, a conclusion reached by a recent analysis by the National Academy of Sciences.

Finally, said Dr. Kistiakowsky, women are simply made to feel out of place in science. Her conclusion was supported by a Ford Foundation study by Lynn H. Fox on the problems of women in mathematics. When students were asked to choose among six reasons accounting for girls' lack of interest in math, the girls rated this statement second: "Men do not want girls in the mathematical occupations."

A friend of mine remembers winning a Bronxwide mathematics competition in the second grade. Her friends—both boys and girls—warned her that she shouldn't be good at math: "You'll never find a boy who likes you." My friend continued nevertheless to excel in math and science, won many awards during her years at the Bronx High School of Science, and then earned a full scholarship to Harvard. After one year of Harvard science, she decided to major in English.

When I asked her why, she mentioned what she called the "macho mores" of science. "It would have been O.K. if I'd had someone to talk to," she said. "But the rules of comportment were such that you never admitted you didn't understand. I later realized that even the boys didn't get everything clearly right away. You had to stick with it until it had time to sink in. But for the boys, there was a payoff in suffering through the hard times, and a kind of punishment—a shame—if they didn't. For the girls it was O.K. not to get it, and the only payoff for sticking it out was that you'd be considered a freak."

Science is undeniably hard. Often, it can seem quite boring. It is unfortunately too often presented as laws to be memorized instead of mysteries to be explored. It is too often kept a secret that science, like art, takes a well-developed esthetic sense. Women aren't the only ones who say, "I hate science."

That's why everyone who goes into science needs a little help from friends. For the past ten years, I have been getting more than a little help from a friend who is a physicist. But my stepdaughter—who earned the highest grades ever recorded in her California high school on the math Scholastic Aptitude Test—flunked calculus in her first year at Harvard. When my friend the physicist heard about it, he said, "Harvard should be ashamed of itself."

What he meant was that she needed that little extra encouragement that makes all the difference. Instead, she got that little extra discouragement that makes all the difference.

"In the first place, all the math teachers are men," she explained. "In the second place, when I met a boy I liked and told him I was taking chemistry, he immediately said: 'Oh, you're one of those science types.' In the third place, it's just a kind of a social thing. The math clubs are full of boys and you don't feel comfortable joining."

In other words, she was made to feel unnecessary, injurious and out of place.

A few months ago, I accompanied a male colleague from the science museum where I sometimes work to a lunch of the history of science faculty at the University of California. I was the only woman there, and my presence for the most part was obviously and rudely ignored. I was so surprised and hurt by this that I made an extra effort to speak knowledgeably and well. At the end of the lunch, one of the professors turned to me in all seriousness and said: "Well, K. C., what do the women think of Carl Sagan?" I replied that I had no idea what "the women" thought about anything. But now I know what I should have said: I should have told him that his comment was unnecessary, injurious and out of place.

Cole, K. C. "Women in Science." *The Compact Reader*, Second Edition. Jane E. Aaron, Editor. St. Martin's Press, 1987, pp. 274–277. ISBN: 312-15308-2.

Suggestions for discussion and writing:

1. What is Cole's purpose for writing the article?
2. What does Cole perceive as the basic cause of women's lack of scientific background?
3. What is the tone of Cole's language?
3. Discuss the appropriateness of Cole's essay in terms of the twentieth-century.
4. Write a brief essay in which you list the causes and effects of limiting people in a given activity.

THE WRITING PROCESS

APPLICATION:

Having knowledge of the various modes for effective dynamic writing, it only remains for the writer to apply that theoretical information to some practical use. This is accomplished when the writer decides to develop a composition. To aid the writer in the application of his theoretical wisdom, the following is offered as a preliminary guide to getting started.

BRAINSTORMING:

The first thing the writer ought to do in order to develop a composition is **think!** He should find a serious and suitable topic and then brainstorm. The writer next needs to **move the abstract** ideas from his head **to a concrete format** such as a piece of paper. There are several different ways he can achieve this:

1. **focused free writing;**
2. **listing;**
3. **clustering;.**
4. **questioning.**

When using **focused free writing** the writer should center his attention upon the subject matter selected. He should start writing freely without fear of grammatical errors or misspellings. He should write whatever comes to mind for five to fifteen minutes remembering to concentrate only on the topic.

The **listing** technique is similar in that the writer simply lists all the ideas that come to mind for five to fifteen minutes, much like compiling a shopping list. He should mark down everything regardless of how ridiculous, so as to capture his thoughts on paper.

The **clustering** method of brainstorming is best for people who retain strong mental images. Start with the topic written inside a circle, and then slowly develop small circles that include related ideas branching off from the original circle. Group the circles that contain corresponding ideas into clusters that shoot off from the main circle.

The use of **questioning** is yet another way of brainstorming. The old journalistic questions of **who, what, when, where, and why** are very practical tools that a writer can use to develop his ideas. This method is very useful for writing reports and essays.

The most important aspect of brainstorming is to write freely without worrying about grammar. The more ideas the writer has, the more he can use. He should jot down on paper whatever comes to mind regarding the topic of choice. It is not important whether the ideas are profound or ridiculous, it is, however, important that the writer move the ideas from the abstract imagination onto a concrete sheet of paper so that they are readily manageable. This process, called brainstorming, should not take more than twenty minutes.

Next, the writer needs to sort or classify those ideas into some form of grouping. He may, as already discussed, cluster the ideas by placing related concepts into small groups. Another method is to divide the ideas by similarity and then group them into blocks. For example, a topic about air pollution might look something like this:

Winds —	prevailing high velocity jet stream

Factories —	profits responsibility government control

```
┌─────────────────────────────────────────┐
│                    acids                  │
│                    gases                  │
│        Chemicals —  oxides                │
│                    benzines               │
└─────────────────────────────────────────┘
```

THESIS STATEMENT:

The very best way to separate and categorize the brainstorming material is to develop a thesis statement. This can be achieved quickly and easily by applying the following formula:

Take the topic
add   1. a major point;
           2. a second major point;
           3. a third major point;

and make them all into one sentence written in the third-person.

Example:
Topic — air pollution
add   1. winds
           2. factories
           3. chemicals

and convert into the following thesis:

Air pollution is a major environmental problem caused by prevailing *winds* that capture and spread hazardous wastes which are released by *factories* as *chemical* by-products.

Once the writer has brainstormed and organized the material into a thesis statement, he then is ready to apply it to some sort of a basic framework for essay development.

FRAMEWORK:

There is a basic framework for any essay or composition. It consists of a *beginning*, a *middle*, and an *end*. Such a framework is useful for a writer who is not sure where or how to begin a written composition. The beginning is known as the *introduction*, and it is used by the writer to announce the main idea. The middle is called the *body*, and this is where the writer develops the main idea fully. The end is known as the *conclusion*, and this is the point where the writer advances the main idea of the composition to some final resolution.

Schematically, the framework is structured as follows:

I. Introduction
    A. Thesis statement
    B. Background material
II. Body
    A. Causes
    B. Effects
    C. Solutions
III. Conclusion
    A. Restate the thesis
    B. Discuss the main points of the thesis briefly along with the causes, effects, and solutions
    C. Discuss the consequences and advantages of the proposed solutions, and render an informed opinion.

This framework will prove useful for either the beginning or the experienced writer as a starting point for a composition. To enhance the framework even more, the writer should discuss the topic in terms of *economics*, *politics*, and *social aspects*. Including these three items as a background for the subject will ensure that the writer has touched on areas that are of interest to any reasonable audience.

OUTLINE:

An outline is employed by the writer much like a blueprint is utilized by an architect. It is used by the practical writer to plan out the entire composition step-by-step. He employs it as a guide to follow during the writing stages.

There is a generally accepted format for outlines that are structured in such a way as to show the relevant significance of the various elements of the entire composition. The basic outline is divided into four different areas of importance:

Roman numerals are used to designate the major divisions of the essay;

Capital letters are employed to indicate subdivisions of the major areas;

Arabic numbers are applied to indicate a further subdivision of the capital letters;

Small case letters are employed to denote an even further subdivision of related, but somewhat less important materials.

Each division is designated by a symbol which represents value of importance:

I.   is more important than **A.**

A.   is more important than **1.**

1.   is more important than **a.**

a.   is the least important.

The following is a sample outline for an essay about air pollution:

AIR POLLUTION PLANS BOUND TO FAIL

Thesis: Although various plans have been proposed to *eliminate air pollution, national politics* and a lack of *public support* have allowed *industry* to continue hazardous practices, and consequently all plans inevitably meet with a *complexity* of interest that insure failure.

  I.   Eliminating air pollution

      A.   All plans are costly

      B.   Plans are too complex

 II.   National politics

      A.   Ideology

          1.   Republicans

          2.   Democrats

             a.   Liberals

             b.   Conservatives

      B.   Big business

III. Public support
- A. Environmental groups
- B. Grassroots groups

IV. Industry
- A. Profits vs. loss
- B. Public image
- C. Governmental intrusion

V. Complexity
- A. Legal authority
  1. State
  2. National
  3. International
- B. Cooperation
  1. Problems at international level
  2. Who will bear cost?
  3. Different national perspectives

VI. Conclusion
- A. Elimination of air pollution plans will not work because of national politics, lack of public support, industry's profit motives, complexity of interests, costs, and lack of state, national, and international cooperation
- B. Bipartisan politics are needed.
- C. Public must support environmental plans
- D. Industry must coooperate and comply
- E. Formation of international environmental council
- F. Development of resources to defray costs
- G. Dire future consequences if viable plans are not formulated today.

This is only a sample of many possible outlines. The importance of an outline is that it is used to serve the writer as a guide for planning space, time, and concepts in the written form. A writer may decide, for example, to write a 3,000 word essay. He can utilize the basic outline framework to allocate any specified amount of words to a given area of his plan. Using the sample outline as an example, it is a simple matter to divide six (the six Roman numerals) into 3,000 (the amount of words) and arrive at 500 words per Roman numeral. The writer now knows that he can apportion approximately 500 words for each major section preceded by a Roman numeral, but he also can see that some sections include more elements than others. Because of that, he may decide to allocate 300 words to section I., 700 words to section II., 500 to section III., and so forth, depending upon the size of each section. The writer can further apportion words by dividing the 500 words into each sub-section, 500 words divided by sub-sections A. and B. equal 250 words for each. This type of word allocation in an outline, although seemingly awkward for the beginning writer, is actually a most pragmatic way to plan a composition.

One may similarly allocate time frames through use of the outline. If, for example, the writer has to write an essay in sixty minutes, he can apportion ten minutes for each section of the outline and finish the essay exactly on time. This type of time planning is particularly useful for students who have to write in-class essay examinations within a specified time frame.

The primary use of an outline is for the benefit of the writer. It should be used as a guide or a previously planned schematic of what the writer intends to compose. Sometimes the writer may show it to a boss or a professor for feedback. At other times the writer can use it over a prolonged period as a sort of memory-jogger regarding what he had in mind. Other writers may also utilize the outline because of the clarity and ease with which it may be followed. The truly effective and intelligent writer will not write a composition without first having planned and produced a basic outline.

TECHNICAL WRITING

The technical writing process is used primarily by professionals to communicate in a formal and common fashion.

THE COMMUNICATION PROCESS:

The basic communication process at a given point in time is as follows:

Sender — the one who originates the message

Message — what is conceived

Encoding— the process of phrasing the message

Channel — the means chosen to transmit the message

Noise — anything that interferes with the message

Receiver — the one who accepts the message

Decoding— the process of interpretation

Feedback— the reaction to the message which in itself is a new message

Sender:

The writer needs to consider his role as the sender. For example, when an individual is seeking a job, he most often will consider dress as an important part of sending a message to a potential employer. The same is true in the written form. Think carefully about how the message will appear. The way a sender prepares the message will establish his credibility. The execution of the message is equally important. Be authoritative, and be knowledgeable. Send the message simply and honestly!

Message:

Conceiving and encoding or phrasing the message is crucial to delivering it. Organization, length, level of language, images and symbols, as well as style of transmission, can send either the wrong message or the correct one. Be particularly considerate while encoding.

Channel:

The channel is the means by which the message is sent. Radio, television, telephone, books, and word of mouth are all viable channels for the transmission of a message. Some channels are better than others for sending messages. For example, television has the benefit of the visual and the audio, while the telephone is restricted to the audio. For the handsome movie star, television is clearly the better channel for delivering a message, while to the average looking person, the telephone might suffice best.

Noise:

There are *mechanical* and *semantic* barriers that can interfere with the transmission of a message. For example, noise often occurs in the environment at the time of transmission. A bell ringing or an ambulance siren can distract or interfere with the receivers hearing the total message. This is mechanical noise. Semantic noise happens when there is a difference in the background of the sender and the receiver such as age, education, gender, race, religion, and other cultural aspects. For example, "Let's go shopping," may mean something quite different to a female and a male. For the male, it might simply be the idea of buying something, while to the female it may mean enjoying an outing for the day. Both very often receive two distinctly different messages from the single words, "Let's go shopping." Physical stress and psychological problems can also interfere with the successful transmission of messages. It is important for the writer to consider these noises when encoding his message.

Receiver:

Understanding the audience is a crucial part of sending a successful message. Design your communication to reach a particular audience. To say to a badly behaved four-year old child that "There are certain manifestations of your behavior that are abominable," would be a waste of time because the child's language capacity has not reached that level of understanding. To communicate to the average four-year child it might be better to say "You are not behaving" or "You are not being good." The writer should make sure the audience understands his intention. A teacher may upgrade the level of his language with the intention of his students developing their vocabularies, and thereby expanding their knowledge. The students might misinterpret the new language as something pedantic or high-class, and designed to humiliate through the difference in education between them and the teacher. Such a case would be a positive message received as a negative. The most important step in the communication process is for the sender to carefully consider the receiver.

Decoding:

People use symbols and images to conceive and translate messages. It is important to use symbols and images that have meaning for the receiver. The good writer will define terms, and often use examples to explain them. A nickel bag in a grocer's terms is quite different from a nickel bag in the jargon of the streets. The same symbols, "a nickel bag," can be encoded one way and decoded another. This is also known as interpretation.

Feedback:

Feedback can provide clues as to whether or not the first message was received and decoded properly. Even though feedback is actually an entirely new message in its own right, it is a valuable tool for reformulating or adding something to the original message when it needs to be sent again. Watching an audience can offer much by way of feedback. A look of disgust can indicate a negative reception, while a smile or a nodding head may imply acceptance. Watching, listening, and reading are good ways to measure feedback.

TECHNICAL DEFINITIONS:

Technical definitions are more complex than ordinary definitions, and present special problems of clarity and understanding in the business world. Writing, of the technical type, does not appear in the forms of essays or short stories, and the writer does not have the same space with which to develop ideas fully. Brevity, by necessity in business, is the rule. The practical writer should be familiar with the following:

Simple Definition
Expanded Definition
Point of View Definition

Simple Definition:

A simple definition is a statement that contains only the minimum words necessary to explain the meaning and the essence of the term. The simple definition contains the **term, the genus, and the differentia.** The genus is the part used to indicate a classification that includes the term while the differentia is used to discriminate between the term and the other components of the genus. For example, an FM (differentia) radio (genus) is a transmitting device that functions on a frequency modulation band. The good writer will always strive to base a definition on a clear understanding of the essential nature of the object for which the term stands.

Expanded Definition:

A simple definition, although logical and complete, may not always be useful for explaining the nature of something. When that occurs the use of an expanded definition is in order. A good practical writer will want to define all the possible meanings and implications contained in a given item or subject. The writer will need to employ Example/Illustration in order to make the definition more concrete, and to clarify its full scope of meaning. He must be careful to select just the proper examples and illustrations that are best representative of the subject for definition.

Comparison and Contrast is also a functional mode employed when expanding a definition. It can be used to discriminate between terms which might lead to confusion. For example, the terms "affect" and "effect" are both similar in the sense that a result is usually involved. The writer can use comparison and contrast to show their differences as well as their similarities, and thereby bring about an expanded definition. To produce an expanded definition a writer must use a combination of modes.

Point of View Definition:

The sociologist, psychologist, and attorney may all have a different point of view when referring to an insane person. The sociologist might perceive the insane person as one outside the norms of social behavior, while the psychologist may define the same individual as psychotic, and the attorney may only use the idea of knowing right from wrong to discriminate in his definition of the insane person. What one person may call dirt, another may refer to as earth, and yet another may call it soil, while still another may term it ground. Point of view, language selection, and cultural background, can all add to confusion in defining terms.

The practical writer will establish what is known as a universe of discourse, which simply means, he will decide what the term represents, give an example, and from that point on, the term will have only that particular meaning. In this way, the sender and the receiver can share the same point of view, and thereby facilitate understanding.

TECHNICAL DESCRIPTIONS:

Technical descriptions differ from literary descriptions in the aspect of fact and objectivity. While literary descriptions are used by writers to create dominant impressions, technical descriptions are used to report facts. Technical descriptions are usually part of a longer paper, such as an insurance report where the description is offered as a means for determining how to settle damages. For example, when an automobile accident leaves the vehicle in a state of inoperation, the description of the automobile can be used by the adjusters to determine whether it would be cheaper to repair the vehicle or to give the claimant a cash settlement.

A technical description may also be used by a writer who wishes to show some newly developed product, machine part, or a process, and how it operates or may be useful within a given context. This type of description is most useful in the business world.

The writer may want to describe an object or a process as a whole. To do this he needs to include:

a definition of the object or process;

an explanation of the manner in which it performs its function;

a general description of the object or process;

a list of its major components or steps.

The definition of an object or a process is a simple straight forward explanation of its essence. The explanation of its function need not be extensive, but it ought to be detailed enough so as to give a good idea as to the way it works. The general description of the object or process should be presented in such a way so that the reader receives an overall view before he sees its more intricate parts or phases. A list of major components will suffice to permit the reader to gain a comprehensive understanding of the general composition of the object or the process.

To make sure that the description is complete, the writer should offer a description of the functional parts or steps in conjunction with their overall relevance to the object or the process. This is where the purpose for the item or process and the characteristics that allow it to achieve its purpose are shown to the reader.

All of this should be followed by a brief conclusion in which the writer presents an overall impression of the object or process and its functional purpose.

CORRESPONDENCE:

Letter writing is an essential part of the business world as well as everyday life in general. Technical letter writing is focused generally upon things and ideas rather than people. This requires a succinct style of writing in order to communicate in a clear manner. All letters should be written in a courteous and positive tone. One of the most important aspects of technical letters is the form. Next in importance is the substance of the correspondence. Given that information the practical writer should make sure to include the following in every letter written:

Heading
Address
Salutation
Body
Zipper Clause
Complimentary Close
Signature

Heading:

The heading is the part that shows the address of the writer and the date. Headings are handled differently, depending upon whether the letter has a banner or not (see examples A and B, p. 161–162).

Address:

This is used to show to whom the letter is addressed.

Salutation:

The salutation is the "Dear Sir" part of the letter. Use the appropriate title for the person being addressed. End the salutation with a colon. If the reader is an acquaintance use a comma.

Body:

This is the main part of the letter. The body should be almost centered with equal margins on both sides. Usually, there will be a bit more blank space showing at the bottom of the letter than at the top. This gives the correspondence a clean visual appearance.

Zipper Clause:

The zipper clause is the "if any questions please contact me" section of the letter. This part is very important should it become necessary to enter into litigation. This clause is documentation of the fact that the writer has left open an avenue for discussion regarding any problems that may arise, while the respondent conversely has chosen to close or "zip up" the communication by not responding; a key point in legal actions.

Close:

This is the "Sincerely," part of the letter. The complimentary close usually ends with "Sincerely," or "Respectfully," as a courteous way to conclude the letter.

Signature:

This is where the writer signs in longhand with the typed version of the signature below. Signing a letter is a legal commitment and a statement that the writer understands all that has been written.

The stationery should be of good quality, unruled bond paper. The usual business letter is on eight and one-half inches wide by eleven inches long paper. When the first page of a two-page letter is on company letterhead, then the second page should be blank, and of equal quality and color as the first page.

There are two distinctly different forms for letters depending on whether they have letterheads or not. Most business correspondence is written in the block form. The following two examples are designed to demonstrate how to write the appropriate form for each type:

Example A — with letterhead

BANNER

July 15, 1995

Mr. Edward Connors
Counselor
Bison State College
91 Johnson Park
Buffalo, New York 14201

Dear Mr. Connors:

Thank you for the information regarding Bison State College. Your prompt reply is most appreciated.

I hope that you will be able to arrange the visit to the Bison State College campus this coming November 16, 1995 so that the students of Lackawanna High School may see all of the facilities first-hand. As you know, they are very excited about the prospect of college, and your recommendation is most important in their final selections.

I shall telephone you next week on Monday to arrange a schedule that is mutually convenient for the November visit. Should you have any questions please feel free to contact me at 716-878-5419.

Thank you for your time and consideration in this matter.

Sincerely,

Patricia McNaney, Counselor
Lackawanna High School

Example B — without letterhead

882 Carney Street
Baltimore, Maryland 84420
February 1, 1995

Ms. Susan L. Bosley
Detroit Educational Services, Inc.
3300 Broadway
Detroit, Michigan 22310

Dear Ms. Bosley:

Thank you for your letter of December 16, 1994 inviting me to serve as a member of Detroit Educational Services, Inc.

I am honored to accept your invitation to serve as a member of the organization. I have long admired the work of the agency, and am delighted to now become a part of it. Please advise me of how I may serve. Should you have any questions please contact me at 716-854-6693.

Thank you again for the invitation. I look forward to my tenure as a member of Detroit Educational Services, Inc.

Sincerely,

Kristopher Bratt

There are several different types of letters that a writer will want to send over a lifetime. *The Lifetime Encyclopedia of Letters* by Harold E. Meyer, published by Prentice-Hall in 1983 is an excellent reference for any type of letter a writer may wish to compose, ranging from a simple thank you to the more sophisticated how to return a gift. For the purpose of business, however, there are only two other letters of major importance, the letter of inquiry and letter of complaint.

Letter of Inquiry:

This letter is written in a standard correspondence format. It should include the following:

1. a clear statement of the purpose for gaining information and the subject of the information requested;
2. an explanation of why and when the information is needed;
3. an explanation of why this particular agency was selected and the benefits for responding;
4. the questions the respondent is expected to answer;
5. an offer to compensate for any costs involved;
6. an expression of appreciation for the respondent's time and effort;
7. a zipper clause for protection against the possibility of legal action.

Letter of Complaint:

This letter should be written in a standard correspondence format. It should include:

1. a courteous statement regarding the facts of the complaint;
2. an explanation of how the writer has been damaged or inconvenienced;
3. what the writer wishes of the respondent in terms of compensation or adjustment;
4. how it is to the respondent's advantage to honor the complaint;

5. an acknowledgment of the respondent's powers of reason, and of his moral and legal responsibility;

6. a zipper clause for protection against the possibility of legal action.

REPORTS, MEMOS, PROPOSALS, AND PRESENTATIONS:

There are four major functions of technical communication. When preparing a report, memo, letter, proposal, or presentation the emphasis ought to be designed to:

> **inform**
> **instruct**
> **persuade**
> **document**

Any communication may serve several or all of the functions, but remember that function should influence form.

To inform:

Function dictates form. To compile a directory, for example, the writer may wish to list things alphabetically or according to some particular title or office. To assemble a dictionary, however, the writer is almost required to put it into alphabetical order because that is the way most readers will approach a dictionary. It is important to remember that when informing, the writer wants to:

1) call attention to data
2) have it interpreted correctly
3) have it accepted
4) have it stored for later retrieval.

To instruct:

To get the reader to do something it is necessary to provide some simple step-by-step procedure that he may follow. Let the purpose influence the form. One can use words or pictures as a means for instruction, depending upon the background of the audience.

To persuade:

Logic and reason, along with an emotional appeal, will generally serve to persuade the reader to some way of thinking or to some action or change of behavior. Good argument and a rational presentation are the key components to successful persuasion.

To document:

Documentation is one of the most important aspects of technical communication. Next to keeping records for later retrieval, it is sometimes necessary to provide evidence of some event or idea. For example, in a court of law, an attempt to pay for damages is a crucial element in determining responsibility. Did the defendant attempt to resolve the problem before coming to court? The presentation of a letter pre-dating the court appearance as proof of the defendant's intention to resolve the situation by paying for damages, very often will work in his favor. In such circumstances, the documentation can serve as evidence.

Reports:

Reports can differ widely in form and length. Most important, however, is the fact that they are designed to convey information to someone or some agency because it is the responsibility of the writer to do so. The key word is *responsibility*, for a written piece is only a report when the author is communicating as a matter of responsibility. Reports are vital for the successful operation of business and governmental organizations, as they are the primary means for informing the management and high executives of the progress of a given aspect of the organization. From these reports decisions are made regarding future activity.

The practical writer should strive to include accuracy and detail in all reports. Anyone ought to be able to read them and understand them without relying upon a dictionary or special skills. Most of all, the writer should provide what is needed in order for the reader to have a comprehensive understanding of the content. The writer should make sure that the report is interesting, thorough, free from irrelevant material, free from bias, and above all, objective.

There are reports that are lengthy and complex, and written in a very formal style. These are called formal reports.

Formal Reports:

Formal reports should include:

> **Covering Memorandum**
> **Title Page**
> **Table of Contents**
> **Headings**
> **Summary**
> **Introduction**
> **Conclusion**
> **Appendix**
> **Bibliography**

The order of the formal report may appear odd to the average writer, yet, for purposes of business, this is the manner in which most reports and proposals are written. Following this sequence permits the decision-makers to see the report in the order of importance from their respective points of view.

Covering Memorandum:

The writer identifies the report, makes reference to the subject of the report, and the reason for reporting about the subject. This covering memorandum is where the writer may place any pertinent materials that may not be included in the report proper.

Title Page:

The title page is used to indicate the subject of the report, the person or agency to whom the report is made, the person or agency making the report, and the date of the report.

The following is a sample title page:

Example C

DEPARTMENT OF BIOLOGY
Report 664

THE EFFECTS OF ZEBRA MUSSELS IN LAKE ERIE
A Case Study of Lake Erie, Buffalo, N.Y.

by
Craig G. Werner
Patricia Dare
Rand R. Roberts

Published by the
Department of Biology
May 26, 1995

State University of New York   Buffalo, New York

Table of Contents:

The table of contents is similar to the table found in a book. It includes the introduction, summary, body material, recommendations, appendixes, and other detailed data. Indentations show the order of importance.

Headings:

These are most valuable when compiling formal reports. When employed properly, they can be used by a reader to separate important materials. They can be used to demonstrate the general design of the report, and they should correspond with the indentation order of the table of contents.

Summary:

This section is useful in terms of letting the reader know what to expect in the total report. It serves as a sort of introduction, except the reader also gets to view the completed idea before reading the entire report. Brief abstracts may be used in place of a summary. The main idea is to inform the reader of the total information in just a few hundred words.

Introduction:

As with any other type of introduction it should include comments about the subject as a whole, a specific thesis, background information, the general design of the report, and some comments designed to create interest.

Conclusion:

The conclusion should include the results and any recommendations. This should be written on the basis of evidence and logical projections based on the contents found within the body, rather than the ordinary ending found in most conclusions.

Appendix:

An appendix is useful for placing pertinent material outside the main body of the report. Letters, graphs, photographs, and the like are materials that should be studied by themselves. They may be referred to in the body of the report by indicating "see appendix A" but they are not part of the interior report. An appendix is useful for handling supporting materials in a formal report.

Bibliography:

The bibliography is a standard way to list references.

Remember that the best way to prepare a report is to:
1. **brainstorm the subject;**
2. **form a plan and an outline;**
3. **gather data, analyze, and interpret;**
4. **prepare maps, tables, and statistics;**
5. **write first draft;**
6. **revise;**
7. **write final draft paying attention to all the formal details.**

Memos:

There are short reports which come in the form of letters and memoranda. These are known as non-formal reports. When a report does not include maps, statistics, and graphs, it need only be communicated in letter form. A non-formal report may also be written in memorandum form. Similar to a letter, the memorandum differs only in the heading. The heading usually appears this way:

To:
From:
Date:
Subject:

A memorandum is generally sent within an organization, and written and read on company time. Time is money; therefore, be brief when writing a memorandum. Do not write salutations or complimentary materials. When designing a memorandum, remember to ask questions such as:

Why is this information needed?

How much is already known about the situation?

How much will be understood?

What should be done with this information?

A memorandum is designed to record and convey information laterally or vertically within an organization as well as to serve as the basis for decision-making.

Proposals:

A proposal is one of the most important items a writer can prepare in the business world. Many times promotion, salary increase, and sometimes employment, can hinge on the successful proposal. A proposal is a request for support or a suggestion of an action that should be taken. The proposal is in essence, an offer to do something such as solve a problem or research information. Many business executives hire proposal writers just for the purpose of landing large contracts. Universities and private not-for-profit corporations usually have grant writers who secure funds and endowments by virtue of their skills in writing proposals. Formal proposals are generally written in a specific style.

The following is an example of what should be included in any proposal:

Letter of Transmittal

Title Page

Summary Abstract

Table of Contents

Statement of Request

Problem Statement

History of Problem
Scope of Problem
Methodology
Facilities
Personnel
Advantages and Disadvantages
Duration
Budget
Reports
Evaluations
Future Funding

Letter of Transmittal:

This is a formal letter that is used to identify the proposal, give particulars, and express an interest in providing a service.

Title Page:

A title page is used to identify the proposal. It includes the title of the proposal, the name, title, and address of the person or agency to whom the proposal is submitted, any identifying numbers, dates of submission, money amounts, and the name, title, and address of the person or agency to perform the service.

Summary Abstract:

This is a brief statement of the services to be rendered. It includes an identification of the problem and a proposed solution.

Table of Contents:

This part is written much like the table of contents in a book.

Statement of Request:

This is a statement of who will perform the services, what the services entail, and what the cost will be to provide the services.

Problem Statement:

This is one of the most important sections of any proposal. It is crucial to define the problem accurately, demonstrate that the problem does indeed exist, discuss its ramifications and significance, and show its relevance in terms of a larger order.

History of Problem:

The writer uses this section to describe the causes leading to the problem as well as the effects. This is where a writer often will present a review of the literature regarding the problem in order to demonstrate his total understanding of the nature and scope of the problem.

Scope of Problem:

In this section the writer establishes the limits of the proposed services. Everything written in this part of the proposal needs to be clearly defined.

Methodology:

The methodology is the means by which the services will be carried out. Most proposals include standard methodologies that are used to demonstrate to the reader that they will indeed work.

Facilities:

These are those items used in a physical sense. They can range anywhere from building space to classroom chalkboards, and more simply stated, are those things necessary to provide the proposed services.

Personnel:

People are needed in order to do the work. A listing of the people and their professional credentials is usually placed in this section.

Advantages and Disadvantages:

These ought to be discussed in any proposal. It is important to honestly project what may be in store for the reader, and what he may anticipate by way of results.

Duration:

This is the section designed to show the schedules and time span of the proposed project.

Budget:

The budget is another important part of any proposal. The writer must demonstrate that the expense incurred is justified. Cost benefit analysis is a useful tool in the narrative of this section. The costs are detailed in a budget sheet and itemized under headings such as salaries, travel, supplies, and the like. Remember that it is not the writer's money being used, but the reader's. Show him how his money will be used beneficially.

Reports:

These are used to keep the grantor informed of the progress, and to establish the final results of the proposed project. This section should include a timetable for all reports, with the names and titles of the people responsible for submitting them.

Evaluations:

These are also important if the grantor is to know whether he has received full value for his financial support. Both internal and external evaluations are best. Internal evaluations are methods by which the agency rates the performance of its personnel and facilities in terms of the proposal. External evaluations generally are conducted by outside experts in the field related to the subject of the proposal, and have the extra weight of offering an objective view to the grantor.

Future Funding:

This is important in terms of showing the grantor that the writer has a grasp on the long range consequences of the proposal. It is unrealistic to expect the grantor to continue to pay for any long range project, unless it is possible to show how the proposal writer intends to become self sufficient at some point in time. Grantors do not run a charity business, rather they are interested in receiving some social or financial benefits for their efforts.

Presentations:

Oral presentations are an intricate part of the business world. The presentation of material in the oral form poses special problems with organization, delivery, and most of all, nervousness. Most presentations are made before an audience of interested people. Very often the presenter feels the stress of a public appearance and has difficulty keeping material in order. This is where presentations come into the realm of technical writing. If one wants to make successful presentations, it will be necessary to write the presentation. The most important aspects for writing and making good presentations can be found in the following:

Preparation

Audience

Material Arrangement.

Preparation:

Know the subject thoroughly. Make sure to draw up an outline. Commit the major points to memory. Rehearse the speech privately several times in a natural speaking voice.

Rehearse the speech in front of a small group of family or friends. Edit all unnecessary material. Bear in mind that rehearsal is the key to a successful presentation.

Audience:

Analyze the audience to determine the best method of presentation. Figure out what type of a group the audience is. Determine why the members came together. Decide what the audience members already know, and how they feel about the topic. Ascertain the purpose for the presentation. Is it to persuade the audience to an action or to inform regarding something of interest? The presentation ought to reflect the audience composition in terms of understanding and background.

Material Arrangement:

First, an orientation is in order. The audience should be made aware of what to expect, and how the presentation is planned. Second, arrange the body of the speech in order of importance, much like a written composition. Begin with a strong impression and something to capture interest. Next turn to something less important, and then build from there until reaching a climatic statement or idea. At the conclusion, summarize the material presented so the audience has an overall picture of what was said. Use notes, standard language, and a relaxed style for delivery. Remember to "talk with" the audience about something of importance.

Helpful Hints:

Establish objectives clearly and identify what the members of the audience need to know, why they should know it, and why it is important.

Know the subject thoroughly.

Learn as much as possible about the audience members and then direct everything to them in their language.

Prepare an outline or cue cards to use during the presentation.

Start with an anecdote or humorous story that is relevant to the subject. Create a relaxed mood.

Cover only the material that time will allow.

Use visual aids.

Let the audience know what the main point will be, make it, then summarize it.

Do not memorize or read all the material. Speak as if talking in a normal conversation.

Keep eye contact, making sure to scan the audience looking for individual listeners.

Demonstrate confidence, enthusiasm, and an eagerness to share information.

Change the pace of the delivery in terms of pitch, volume, and tone.

Pause briefly after each key point. Use cues such as "this is important" and "you might want to pay particular attention to this" as a means for making a solid point.

End with a strong closing statement that is positive.

COVER LETTERS, RESUMES, AND CURRICULUM VITAE:

Cover Letters:

The cover letter should be brief and to the point. The writer should begin with a short paragraph indicating the position he is applying for, and where he learned of its availability. He should next identify himself and make it clear that the letter is one of application. The central part of the letter should begin with some item of interest to the potential employer. After that, the writer should work in the areas of educational background, experience, references, and special or unique qualifications that suit the needs of the potential employer. The ending should be arranged to suggest action on the part of the potential employer. A suggestion about calling the secretary in a few days to arrange an appointment or mention of the fact that the writer is readily available for a personal interview often can make the difference between acceptance and rejection.

The following are samples of cover letters:

Example D—Cover Letter

1200 Cleveland Avenue
Saginaw, Michigan 97683
February 18, 1995

Mr. Michael Leonard
Personnel Director
The Sunmaid Fruit Corporation, Inc.
2200 Bradenton Blvd.
Tampa, Florida 89088

Dear Mr. Leonard:

I am applying for the position of Warehouse Manager as advertised in the BRADENTON BUGLE on February 1, 1995. Enclosed you will find a resume and three letters of reference. I believe that after viewing my credentials you will find that I possess the very skills needed to fulfill this very important post.

As indicated in the attached resume, I have worked for the last three years as an inventory clerk at the State University of Montana, Butte Campus. During that time I have come to learn all phases of inventory control, and in particular those areas most related to ordering, receiving, storage and retrieval, and shipping. I am familiar with inter-state rules and regulations regarding the storage and shipment of materials, and also have a working knowledge of employee-employer relations in terms of personnel policies and federal and state laws.

It is my belief that The Sunmaid Fruit Corporation could benefit from my experience in the field of warehousing. Should you agree, I would welcome the opportunity to meet with you at a time most convenient for you in order to discuss my credentials.

Thank you for your time and kind consideration to this letter.

Sincerely,

Ryan Jordan

Enclosures

Example E—Cover Letter

933 Jackson Park
Topeka, Kansas 66615
February 18, 1995

Smith Bothers Electronics
Personnel Manager
235 Ackerman Avenue
Topeka, Kansas 66634

Dear Personnel Manager:

It was recently reported in the TOPEKA SUN-TIMES that your company is opening a plant in the Topeka area. I wish to apply for an entry-level position as a computer assembler at the new plant.

I have a Bachelor's Degree in Information Sciences from the State University of Idaho where I took a wide variety of computer related courses. I served as the utility person in Idaho State's Computer Laboratory where I had the responsibility of maintenance and repair for all the hardware equipment in the lab. Through that experience I have become very knowledgeable about the assembly and workings of computers and other electronic equipment.

I would be happy to meet with you at your convenience and provide you with any additional information you may require. I have enclosed a resume for your perusal along with three letters of reference. I believe that after viewing my credentials you will find that I possess the skills needed to fulfill an entry-level position at your new facility.

Should you have any questions please contact me at the above address or at 622-867-9934.

Thank you for your time and kind consideration to this letter.

Respectfully,

David Wiles

Enclosures: resume, three letters

Resumes:

The practical writer will find it necessary to have a resume to go along with a cover letter. A resume is a factual picture of a writer's background in tabular form. There are various forms of the resume; however, the important thing to remember about a resume is that it is designed to accompany a cover letter, and it frees the letter of basic information that may not be interesting, but which is necessary in relation to the position of employment. In the cover letter, the writer attempts to focus the reader's attention on specific qualifications, while in the resume the writer simply presents a full record of background.

The resume should include:

> **Personal Data**
> **Educational Background**
> **Experience**
> **References**

The following is a sample resume:

Example E—Resume

Kenneth D. Sellers
29 Oxford Street
Lawrence, Massachusetts 09883
815-667-9455

Education:

M.A. English, 3.0 G.P.A.
Boston University
Boston, Mass.
1980–1985

George Washington High School–B avg.
Lawrence, Mass.
1976–1980

Experience:

Kencroft Warehouse, Inc.
276 Military Road
Tonawanda, New York 14222
Title: Laborer
Duties: load and unload trucks,
       store freight
Supervisor: Mr. John Donnely
1980–1984

Salcray Drugstore
335 Mulberry Street
Revere, Mass. 81966
Title: Assistant Manager
Duties: schedule personnel, order stock
Supervisor: Mrs. Carrie Janik
1985–present

References:

Denise McConville
202 Pine Avenue
Revere, Mass. 81966

Lori A. Reyes
22 Larbo Street
Lowell, Mass. 81733

Example G—Resume

Jason D. Simpson

Current Address
29 Oxford Street
Lawrence, Massachusetts 09883
815-667-9455

Permanent Address
16 Tremont Avenue
Burls, Iowa
912-774-9873

Objective: Entry level position leading to Accounting career.

PROFESSIONAL PROFILE
- Highly organized and committed to professionalism.
- Able to handle pressure well, conscious of detail.
- Excellent written, verbal, and inter-personal skills.

ACCOUNTING SKILLS
Profit and loss—income statements—accounts payable payroll—general ledgers and journals—balance sheets computerized accounting, and corporate tax accounting.

PROFESSIONAL EXPERIENCE
Bookkeeper/Data Entry—White, Smith, and Jaekle, Inc. 113 Plaza Pl., Bacon, GA. 1987–present
- Maintained computerized accounts for clients. Worked with IBM compatible computer, Macintosh 404, and VAX main frame linked to New Bedford, MA.

Personnel Manager—Manpower, Inc.
1222 Court Center, Buffalo, NY. 1984–1987
- Responsible for filling customer orders for labor from personnel pool, recruitment, training, health.

EDUCATION
M.S. Business, June 1984
University of Buffalo

References furnished upon request

Curriculum Vitae:

The curriculum vitae, sometimes called the **vita,** is much like the resume, but on a much **larger scale.** Curriculum vitae literally means **course of life.** The curriculum vitae or vita is used when a potential employer wants an **in-depth** look at an applicant's **background.** The vita usually is structured in this type of format:

> **Mastery of Profession**
> **(educational degrees)**
>
> **Professional History**
> **(work experience)**
>
> **Publications**
>
> **Presentations**
>
> **Special Skills**
>
> **Awards and Recognition**
>
> **Professional Organizations**
>
> **Community Organizations**
>
> **Hobbies and Interest**

The curriculum vitae is *organized like the resume,* except the writer should prepare it in *much more depth.* There are various forms of vita, and the writer should prepare his in a functional manner so as to highlight those aspects of his life of which he is most proud. Most high ranking executives and professionals always *maintain a resume* and a vita which they *up-date* at the beginning of *each new year.*

Samples of the curriculum vitae, which usually range in length from five to fifteen pages, can be found in any local library or in books such as Carl McDaniels' *Developing a Professional Vita or Resume.* (1978) or *Robinson's Resource Guide for Writing Cover Letters, Resumes, and Curriculum Vitae* (1991).

The following is a sample curriculum vitae:

Example H

CURRICULUM VITAE
James G. Ventola, Ph.D.
345 Verplank Drive
Williamsburg, MA
(315) 854-8743

MASTERY OF SUBJECT MATTER

Degrees

> 1990—Ph.D., English, State University of Colorado
> 1986—M.A., English, University of Michigan
> 1980—B.A., English, University of Delaware

Consultations

> Consultant to Dr. Phillip Santa Maria, Associate Vice President of Student Affairs, State University College at Buffalo, for matters pertaining to literacy and language, 1990–1992.

> Consultant to Ms. Paula Ranklin, Director of Literacy Volunteers of America, for development of a literacy program, 1991.

> Consultant to Dr. Charles K. Martin, Director of New State Educational Programs for Adults, regarding adult literacy and equivalency diplomas, 1990–1991.

PROFESSIONAL HISTORY

> University of Maryland, South Campus
> 1300 Elm Street
> Brynard, MD 23365
> Associate Professor of English—1990 to present

> University of Michigan
> 2367 Dearborn Avenue
> Redleaf, MI 43566
> Instructor of English, 1984–1986

James G. Ventola
Page 2

PUBLICATIONS

Books:

Literacy and the American Adult. Needham Heights, Mass.: Simon & Schuster Publishing. 1993.

Practical Writing for Adults. Needham Heights, Mass.: Simon & Schuster Higher Education Group. 1990.

Articles:

"From Burlesque to Boccaccio." *Eclectic Literary Forum.* Summer, 1992. Tonawanda, N.Y.: Elf Associates, Inc., 1992.

"A Vignette." *Portrait.* Spring, 1992. Buffalo, N.Y.: State University College at Buffalo, 1992.

"A Korean Christmas." *New Voices in American Poetry.* New York: Vantage Press, Inc., 1990.

"Semiotic Structures in Literary Study." *Niagara Linguistics Society Journal.* Buffalo, N.Y.: Niagara Linguistic Society, 1989.

"The Magic of Fairy-Tales." *MLA Journal.* Winter, 1988. New York: Modern Language Association, 1988.

Presentations and Papers:

Keynote Speaker, *The Adult and Literature Lecture Series.* University of Michigan, October 21, 1991.

"The Adult Learner." A paper presented to the Education Association of Western New York, Niagara Falls, N.Y., September, 20, 1991.

"A Semiotic Approach to the Fairy-Tale." A paper presented to American Linguistic Association, Berkeley, Cal., July, 15, 1990.

Organizer and Keynote Speaker of The National Literacy Conference: 1989. Sponsored by the Modern Language Association and the University of Michigan, Department of English. Redleaf, Mich., March 14, 1989.

Orwell's *Animal Farm:* An Adult Learner's Perspective. A paper presented to The Association for the Study and Advancement of Non-traditional Learners. Buffalo, N.Y., January 3, 1988.

PROPOSALS AND GRANTS

Princeton University Foundation.
Received funding for the development of a pilot project designed to enhance the delivery of services to adult learners:

1992 $35,000

Greater Buffalo Foundation; Education Division.
Received funding for a literacy development project:

1991 $10,000

University of Michigan Foundation.
Received funding to study the impact of non-traditional students upon traditional students in the classroom setting:

1991 $12,500

New York State Department of Education.
Received funding for a literacy educational component for Daemen College's Higher Education Opportunity Program:

1988 $55,000

PROFESSIONAL ORGANIZATIONS

American Federation of Teachers
Continuing Education Association of Western New
York
International Association for the Study of People
Melville Society, Secretary
Modern Language Association
National Council of Teachers of English
National Education Association
Niagara Linguistics Society, Past President
United University Professions

COMMUNITY ORGANIZATIONS

Alliance for the Mentally Ill
American Rescue Workers of New York
Buffalo Community Housing Resources Board
Citizens Council on Human Relations, Vice President
New York Civil Liberties Union
New York Public Service Interest Group
New State Council for Environmental Issues
Salvation Army, Board Member

MAJOR COMMITTEES

Scheduling Committee. Department of English
University of Colorado, 1990—present

Search Committee. Department of English
University of Colorado, 1990—present

Niagara Linguistics Society Planning Committee
(Ad Hoc) 1989

United Way of Ann Arbor. Allocations Committee
1988–1989

Easter Seals of Michigan Fund Raising Committee
1986–1987

University Wide Affirmative Action Committee 1986

Academic Appeals Committee (student member)
1982

AWARDS, NOMINATIONS, AND RECOGNITION

Summa Cum Laude, University of Delaware

Dean's List each semester

Phillip Wilson Academic Scholarship for highest
GPA

Faculty Merit Award, University of Colorado 1990

President's Award for Excellence in Teaching—1991
University of Colorado—1991

Distinguished Community Service Award—1992
presented by the National Alliance for the Mentally
Ill

COURSES AND EDUCATIONAL DEVELOPMENT

Developed the Boulder Community College Preparation Program for youth and adults returning to
school—1992

The Senior Citizen in Literature. English 431.
University of Colorado—Fall 1992

College Study Skills. English 099.
University of Colorado—Fall 1991

Studies in Semiotics and Language. English 300.
University of Colorado—Spring 1990

Form, Image, and Culture. English 247.
University of Michigan—Spring 1985

CONCLUSION

Now that the reader has been presented with the basic principles, the primary and secondary modes, the fundamental writing process which includes development and application, and the technical writing process, he should be able to use them effectively in order to produce clear, cohesive, and comprehensive compositions. Always bearing in mind the basic principles of *purpose, substance, structure,* and *style,* the reader should now be able to apply the theoretical ideas of exposition, narration, description, argument/persuasion, example/illustration, process analysis, division and classification, observation and inference, comparison and contrast, analogy, and cause and effect, as set forth in this book, to the production of more meaningful and practical written works. This new understanding of the use of practical writing techniques can only serve to make the reader of this book a more effective writer.

REFERENCES

Aaron, Jane E. *The Compact Reader,* Second Edition. New York: St. Martin's Press, 1987.

Alvarez, Joseph A. *Elements of Composition.* New York: Harcourt Brace Jovanovich, Publishers, 1985.

Conlin, Mary Lou. *Patterns Plus,* Third Edition. Boston, Mass.: Houghton Mifflin Company, 1990.

Fitzpatrick, Carolyn H. and Ruscica, Marybeth B. *The Complete Writer's Workbook.* Lexington, Mass.: D.C. Heath and Company, 1988.

Gordon, Helen Heightsman. *Developing College Writing.* New York: St. Martin's Press, 1989.

McQuade, Donald and Atwan, Robert. *Thinking in Writing,* Second Edition. New York: Alfred A. Knopf, 1983.

Meyer, Harold E. *Lifetime Encyclopedia of Letters.* Englewood Cliffs, N.J.: Prentice-Hall, 1983.

Perrin, Robert. *The Beacon Handbook,* Second Edition. Boston, Mass.: Houghton Mifflin Company, 1990.

Robinson, Zan Dale and Patricia M. Robinson's *Resource Guide for Writing Resumes and Cover Letters.* Buffalo, N.Y.: E. W. Connors Publishing Company, 1993.

Rosa, Alfred and Eschholz, Paul. *Models for Writers,* Second Edition. New York: St. Martin's Press, 1986.

Shaw, Harry. *A Complete Course in Freshman English,* Sixth Edition. New York: Harper & Row, 1967.

Troyka, Lynn Quitman and Nudelman, Jerrold. *Steps in Composition*, Fifth Edition. Englewood Cliffs, N.J.: Prentice Hall, 1990.

Tyner, Thomas E. *Discovery: An Inductive Approach to Writing.* New York: St. Martin's Press, 1990.

Webb, Suzanne S. *The Resourcesful Writer*, Second Edition. New York: Harcourt Brace Jovanovich, Publishers, 1990.

GLOSSARY

ABSTRACT

An abstract word refers to an idea, attitude, or quality. Terms such as love, courage, and beauty are examples of abstract words.

ANALOGY

A special form of comparison in which the writer explains something by comparing it to something familiar.

ANTONYM

A word that has an opposite meaning to another word. Love, for example, is the antonym of hate.

ARGUMENT

An objective, rational appeal to an audience regarding an issue or controversial subject. The purpose of using argument is to persuade an audience to agree with a point of view or pursue a particular course of action. There are two basic types of argument. One is persuasive, and used to appeal to emotions, while the other is logical, and employed to appeal to the intellect.

AUDIENCE

The intended reader or readers of a particular written piece. A writer ought to give careful consideration to the elements of bias and expectation, as well as the educational and cultural background of the audience, if he wishes to communicate in an effective manner.

CAUSE AND
EFFECT

The method of development in which the writer assumes that every action or state of being is the result of another action or state of being. The causes are seen as actions that happen, while the effects are discerned as consequences of the actions. Cause and effect reasoning is most useful as a writing mode.

CLASS
A grouping in which items of the same type are placed after division and classification.

CLASSIFICATION AND DIVISION
The breaking down of ideas into component parts. The parts are then explained in detail and classified on the basis of some common characteristic or quality that identifies them as parts of a class.

COHERENCE
Effective and meaningful relations between all parts of a composition. Logical connections among sentences, paragraphs, and parts of the work.

COMPARISON
The writer establishes similarities between subjects drawn from the same class. Comparison is generally used in tandem with contrast.

CONCLUSION
The writer restates the main ideas or central theme and then offers an opinion regarding the significance of the topic. The conclusion usually is placed in the last paragraph of a composition.

CONCRETE
A term used to describe or name a specific object, person, place, or action that can directly be perceived by the senses.

CONNOTATION
The implied or suggested meaning of a word.

CONTRAST
The writer establishes differences between subjects drawn from the same class. Contrast is generally used in tandem with comparison.

DEFINITION	The writer explains the meaning of a term. This can be accomplished through dictionary definitions, or the writer may describe or set limits as to the meaning. This is sometimes called the universe of discourse.
DENOTATION	The direct and explicit definition of a term as set forth in a standard dictionary.
DESCRIPTION	One of the four basic modes used by a writer to explain how a person, place, or thing is perceived by the senses or to show through details how something appears or works.
DETAILS	Specific bits of information such as examples, dates, and incidents that are offered to explain and support the general ideas in a composition.
DEVELOPMENT	An effective composition begins with the writer introducing the main idea, which he then develops through more specific information in the sentences and paragraphs of the essay.
DIALOGUE	Generally found in the narrative mode, dialogue is the conversation between two or more persons, and is used by the writer to give exact wording.
DICTION	The writer's choice of words. Good diction is precise and appropriate in terms of what the writer intends.
DIVISION AND CLASSIFICATION	The breaking down of ideas into component parts. The parts are then explained in detail and classified on the basis of some common characteristic or quality that identifies them as parts of a class.

EFFECT	The result of causes or events. Generally used by writers, in conjunction with the mode of cause and effect, to explain why or how something happens.
EMOTIONAL APPEAL	The part of persuasive argument where the writer employs emotions rather than logic to make a point.
ESSAY	A written composition based upon a thesis. An essay is usually written in three parts: a beginning, middle, and end. The writer attempts to introduce an idea, develop it fully, and render a conclusion.
ETHICAL APPEAL	The part of persuasive argument where the writer employs a sense of moral good, and appeals to the audience's sense of what is right.
EVENT	An occurrence or happening depicted in a composition.
EVIDENCE	The facts or logic used by a writer to support a central argument.
EXAMPLE	A specific illustration of a more general idea or statement used to support an idea.
EXPOSITION	One of the four basic modes used by a writer to clarify, explain, and inform.
EXTENDED DEFINITION	Used by a writer over several sentences or paragraphs to set limits regarding the use of specific terms or concepts.
EXTENDED EXAMPLE	Used by a writer over several sentences or paragraphs to explain complex concepts or statements.

FACTS	Things known with certainty. Used by a writer to support an argument in objective terms.
IMAGE	A written representation of any sensory experience.
INFERENCE	A statement regarding what is still uncertain on the basis of what is certain. An audience will draw an inference based upon material presented in a composition.
LOGICAL APPEALS	The part of persuasive argument where the writer employs reasoning to support his point of view. The writer apeals to the audience's powers of reason and logic to advance his argument.
METAPHOR	A figure of speech used by a writer to compare unlike objects or ideas by attributing the characteristics or qualities of other things to the items being compared.
MIXED MODE	The writer uses a combination of modes to explain, clarify, or advance his major thesis whenever it is impractical or insufficient to employ only one. A writer may, for example, use comparison and contrast mixed with process analysis as a means by which to explain an idea.
MODE OF DEVELOPMENT	The writing technique used to develop the main idea or theme of a composition. Although a writer generally employs combinations of modes during the writing of an essay, he usually applies one particular mode as the primary mode of development.

NARRATION	One of the four basic modes used by a writer to connect related events or experiences together into a meaningful sequence.
OBJECTIVE	A presentation of factual materials without the writer's opinions or biases.
OBSERVATION	A process of discovery wherein the observer notices and analyzes a subject in order to learn as much as possible about its make-up.
OPINION	The writer's belief or conclusion regarding the subject of discussion. Generally the point of the essay where the writer presents his subjective views.
ORDER	The sequence by which the composition is organized. The writer may, for example, structure the essay in a chronological, spatial, or priority order. Chronological would deal with time order, spatial would present physical relations, and priority would be a discussion of points by importance.
PERSON	The writer employs the use of personal pronouns to indicate the narrator of a composition. The first-person pronoun (I, we) is used to indicate that the writer is a participant or observer. The second-person (you) is utilized to address the audience directly. The third-person (he, she, it, one, and they) is applied to provide the audience with an objective view.
PERSUASION	Used to convince the reader, through logical and emotional appeals, to accept the writer's conclusion regarding a given subject. As part of argument, it is one of the four basic modes.

POINT OF VIEW	Determined by the writer's choice of person, time, and tone in the essay.
PROCESS ANALYSIS	The writer employs process analysis to explain how something works or the method used to accomplish something.
PURPOSE	The writer's reason for writing the composition. He may, for example, wish to convince, inform, or instruct an audience.
SIMILE	A figure of speech in which unlike terms are compared. Unlike a metaphor, a simile is usually introduced by words such as "like" or "as."
STYLE	The individual manner a writer chooses to express his ideas.
SUBJECTIVE	A subjective composition is one where the writer expresses his feelings about the subject.
SYNONYM	A word or phrase that has the same meaning as another word or phrase. The writer uses synonyms to clarify unfamiliar terms for the audience.
THESIS	The main or controlling idea of the composition.
THESIS STATEMENT	Technically the proposition of an argument, this is generally placed at the beginning of the composition, and is the main or controlling sentence of the essay.
TIME	Related to point of view, time refers to the present, past, or future action that takes place in the essay.
TONE	The writer's attitude toward his work. It can be humorous, serious, formal, and

informal depending upon the writer's choice.

TRANSITIONS — Words or phrases that the writer employs to link sentences, paragraphs, and larger units of a composition together in order to create cohesiveness.

UNITY — The quality of oneness that results when the writer has successfully related all sentences, paragraphs, and larger units of the composition to the thesis statement.

UNIVERSE OF DISCOURSE — The establishment of definitions so that the writer and the audience have a mutual understanding of the meaning of a word.

AUTHOR AND TITLE INDEX

INDEX